Sadly, since writing his reflection Séamus Heaney died (30th August 2013).
The Irish Hospice Foundation would like to acknowledge and express our deepest
gratitude to Séamus, Marie and their family for their support over the years.

THE GATHERING
REFLECTIONS ON IRELAND

First published in the Republic of Ireland in 2013 by
The Irish Hospice Foundation, Morrison Chambers, 32 Nassau St, Dublin 2, Ireland

Edited by Miriam Donohoe
Project directed by Anne-Marie Taylor
Designed by Steve Averill - AMP Visual

Printed in Ireland by Spectrum Print Logistics.

ISBN: 978 09566590 4 0

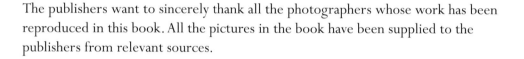

The publishers want to sincerely thank all the photographers whose work has been
reproduced in this book. All the pictures in the book have been supplied to the
publishers from relevant sources.

Front cover photograph: Cyril Byrne / The Irish Times
Members of the 41st Dublin 3rd Port Dalkey Seascouts with the 6th Bebington Eastham
Liverpool Seascouts during their gathering on Dalkey Island.

THE GATHERING
REFLECTIONS ON IRELAND

IN AID OF THE IRISH HOSPICE FOUNDATION

Acknowledgements

Editor: Miriam Donohoe
Project Director: Anne-Marie Taylor
Project Manager: Orla Stafford
Project Assistant: Rebecca Kelly
Design: Steve Averill - AMP Visual
Design Intern: Elizabeth Burgess

Irish Hospice Foundation Team: Kirana Bhagwan, Andy Caffrey, Emer Connolly, Paddy Delaney, Sharon Foley, Denis Hickey, Rebecca Kelly, Caroline Lynch

Special thanks: Kevin Barry, Caroline Erskine, Noirin Hegarty, Vivienne Jupp, Michael Kealy, Mark Keenan, Frank Miller, Jim Miley and the Gathering Ireland 2013 team, Sinead Murphy, Jim O'Brien, Ger Siggins

Media Partner: The Irish Times

Board of the Irish Hospice Foundation: Cynthia Clampett, Denis Doherty, Muiris FitzGerald, Mary Harney, Vivienne Jupp, Cormac Kissane, Jean McKiernan, Antoin Murphy, Margaret Nelson, Kevin O'Dwyer, Michael O'Reilly, Liam O'Siorain, Don Thornhill

Sponsors:

SHARON FOLEY
Foreword

Sharon Foley is Chief Executive of The Irish Hospice Foundation.

Ireland is a nation of story-tellers, and a talent for narrative is part of our heritage. *The Gathering — Reflections on Ireland* is a unique celebration of that heritage, bringing together reflections and recollections from a range of contributors who have all taken different approaches to the overall theme of what it is to be Irish in the world today.

This book originated in a conversation over coffee between Anne-Marie Taylor and me about ideas for a major fundraising project to support the work of the Irish Hospice Foundation (IHF). Published to coincide with *The Gathering 2013*, it is also a memento of this special year, conceived around the idea of inviting the Irish diaspora and descendants 'home' to gather, reconnect, make music, create memories and of course, tell stories, many of which are included. The result is a delightfully varied chronicle of events, experiences and emotions that are informative, uplifting, humorous, poignant and thought-provoking.

Funds raised through this initiative will go towards the IHF's work, and in particular, our pioneering *Design & Dignity* project. The IHF's overall mission is to bring dignity, comfort and choice to all who are facing the end of life. Most people would prefer to die at home, but the reality is that seven out of ten of us will die in healthcare settings. Within these, *Design & Dignity* focuses on the actual physical spaces in which people and their families live out that final journey. This is an aspect of end-of-life care that, while easily over-looked, can significantly influence their experience, for better or for worse.

The provision and sensitive design of appropriate physical spaces – whether a dedicated family room in a hospital, a reflective space in a busy A&E department, or even a mortuary planned with care – can play a key role in enhancing people's sense that their life and the lives of their loved ones are being treated with dignity, care and respect, up to and including the end.

Throughout the world, the hospice movement has been built on the strength of volunteerism, and this book could not have been produced without the commitment of a number of exceptional individuals who have generously volunteered their time and talents to make it possible. I would like to warmly thank our editor, Miriam Donohoe; project director, Anne-Marie Taylor; and designer, Steve Averill, and their families. I also thank each member of the project team and all IHF staff and Board members involved.

Above all, the collaborative nature of this project is shown in the number and variety of contributors, whose response to our request for their participation was overwhelmingly positive. They include well-known names from the worlds of literature, music, art, design, medicine, business, politics and sport, along with working journalists and private individuals. Collectively, they have made this book what it is – a testimony to all that is best in the Irish character, to our capacity for resourcefulness, imagination, generosity of spirit and vision. These are among the qualities that are also driving our *Design & Dignity* project, which, in buying this book, you are helping to support.

Thank you.

MIRIAM DONOHOE
and ANNE-MARIE TAYLOR
Introduction

Miriam Donohoe is a journalist and media consultant.

Anne-Marie Taylor is a freelance management consultant.

Ireland might be a small country on the western edge of Europe, but it continues to have a big impact on the world stage. From the outback in Australia to the missions in Africa, from the plains of South America to the capitals of Europe, and from the islands of Asia to the building sites and office blocks of North America our roots are everywhere.

We are a resilient country that has survived the ravages of famine, civil war, emigration, and recession. Thanks to the indomitable Irish spirit, we have always bounced back. And we have held our heads up high, contributing at home and abroad in a range of fields including the arts, sport, education, business, technology, politics and humanitarian work. This book captures that unique Irish spirit and brings us on an uplifting journey, with inspiring reflections from Irish people and those with Irish connections from all walks of life.

Commander Chris Hadfield, the Canadian astronaut who tweeted as Gaeilge from space, tells of the remarkable bond he forged with Ireland as he orbited the earth; writer Colum McCann writes a special short story; we learn of the courage of Bridget Megarry, who is living with cancer; Riverdance co-creator Moya Doherty shares her rhythm of life with us; RTÉ broadcaster Marian Finucane touches on the theme of emigration; Bono and Séamus Heaney nominate some of their work, and one of our greatest living sportsmen, rugby player Brian O'Driscoll, writes of his passion for his country. And there are many, many more.

There are also emotional and heart-warming stories from some of the thousands of events that were held to mark the year of *The Gathering*: tales of families and friends coming together, re-connecting, and touching on that great Irish spirit which has been the backbone of this country for centuries.

Working on this book has been an enriching and inspiring journey for both of us. The Irish Hospice Foundation's CEO, Sharon Foley, and her dedicated team are a joy. A very special thanks to our project assistant, Rebecca Kelly, for her trojan work – always carried out with great grace and humour, and without whom this book would not have made it to bed!

Finally, a big 'thank you' to all our contributors – those who wrote reflections, those who shared stories from their *Gathering* events, and the professional and amateur photographers who were so generous in allowing us to reproduce their pictures. Between you, you have all helped capture Ireland and its unique spirit in this very special book. We have no doubt that this spirit will continue to stand us in good stead and help us to drive on and scale new heights as a nation.

CONTENTS

THE MAKING OF A 'PEOPLE'S PROJECT'

A reflection by Jim Miley

Jim Miley is the Project Director of The Gathering Ireland 2013.

"So what exactly is this *Gathering* thing about?" That was the question most often asked of me when I first took the helm at 'Ireland's biggest ever tourism project' in spring 2012. A party! A concert! A giant one-day national jamboree! People had all sorts of ideas about what *The Gathering* was.

The first challenge was to create public awareness, to garner the support of communities and to get the nation behind the project. This was more than a tourism promotion. It was clear we would need some help.

To achieve the target of more than 300,000 extra visitors, we set about building what became a 'coalition of the willing'. Local authorities, under the leadership of County and City Managers, provided the spine of the national framework for *The Gathering*, with designated Gathering Co-ordinators appointed in each city and county. Local Steering Groups were formed, with community leaders drawn from a myriad of organisations – tourism interests and those directly involved with the travel trade; business, farming and community groups; music, cultural and arts organisations; a network of individuals and groups all rallying to a common cause.

From early summer 2012, a series of public meetings were held throughout the country. There were some fears. Would anyone show up? How would the media react? Would public cynicism hold sway against a government-sponsored initiative at a time of unprecedented economic austerity?

The fears proved unfounded. Almost 10,000 people attended close to 70 public meetings over a four-month period across every county in Ireland. The meetings generated a wave of ideas for creating local 'gatherings'. There was everything from family and clan gatherings, school reunions, sports, cultural and music events, to a variety of community events, large and small. There were no bounds to people's creativity and imagination – everything from the 'Town of a Thousand Beards' and the 'Red Head Convention' to the 'Irish Wolfhounds Gathering' or the 'Gathering of Golfing Insomniacs'! It was as if *The Gathering* was providing a beacon of positivity and encouragement at a time of great economic and social stress in the country.

In September 2012, around 35,000 American football fans helped to launch *The Gathering* to an American audience as they arrived for the Navy v Notre Dame football game. The event was broadcast live on CBS TV. An RTE series followed Brendan Grace, Bressie and other celebs on a *Gathering* 'Homeward Bound' journey back to their home towns to explore what plans were afoot there. Postcards were dropped through every letterbox in the country, encouraging people to invite their own friends and relatives for *The Gathering.* Some 4,000 and more gathering events were in the making.

The Gathering had already built a formidable support base by late autumn 2012, when a famous Irish-born Hollywood actor challenged the project, describing it as a 'shake-down' and a 'scam'. The criticisms attracted huge national and international media attention. Everyone had a view, as *The Gathering* became a major focal point of public discourse. An array of well-known commentators and celebrities came out to support *The Gathering*, but it was the response from ordinary people that was really telling.

The reaction from one man at a public meeting that I attended in Westmeath in the week after the media storm was typical. "*The Gathering* is about us – our people, our community – and provides us with a platform to reach out to our friends and connections overseas. Now, what can be wrong with that?" he said.

It was at that moment that I knew that *The Gathering* would be a success. Somewhere along the way, it had been transformed from a state-backed idea or concept into a 'people's project'. Even before the first day of *The Gathering* arrived, and long before we could measure the tourism impact in terms of the visitor count, it was apparent that ordinary people in communities and towns across Ireland had taken this idea and shaped it into something relevant to their local area. Tens of thousands of people have worked tirelessly to create thousands of gatherings. They'll certainly have brought visitors to every corner of Ireland, but more importantly, they have helped lift the mood and spirit of the nation in a unique way.

And what of the longer term benefits, *The Gathering's* legacy? There are certainly a number of key gathering events that can be run again in 2014 and in future years, bringing a lasting benefit to the local tourism offering. The *Tóstal* event, a similar concept to *The Gathering*, run 60 years ago in 1953, spawned events such as the All Ireland Drama Festival and Cork International Choral Festival, which continue to thrive today. There is no doubt that similar successes will emerge from *The Gathering.*

But the legacy is much greater than that. The real benefit of *The Gathering* is the way in which it has provided an opportunity to extend and deepen relationships with the diaspora, our friends and ancestral relatives overseas, in a meaningful way. Those relationships are personal and revolve around individual citizens, families and communities. Through *The Gathering* those personal bonds have been strengthened, in some cases, and in others forged for the first time. That has a real and lasting benefit, not only to the individuals, families and communities involved, but also to Ireland as a whole and its extended global family.

The real opportunity now is to continue to nurture our global diaspora relationships on an ongoing basis. In that sense, *The Gathering* doesn't really stop on 31st December 2013, but continues each and every year.

It is particularly appropriate that this collection of gathering stories and reflections on Ireland is in support of the Irish Hospice Foundation. The original meaning of the word 'hospice' or 'hospitium' is a 'rest house for travellers'. In 2013, the Irish people got an opportunity through *The Gathering* to show that Ireland has the capacity to be a very special rest house for travellers, one where the welcome mat was that little bit more inviting and the experience all the more special. To all of those in Ireland who made that special effort to 'Be part of it', we say a big thank you. You made it what it was. And, to our friends from around the globe who came to visit, we invite you to come 'gather' with us again.

THE FAMINE ATTIC GATHERING
Marese McDonagh

In the spring of 1849, when Ireland was still in the grip of the Great Famine, 15-year-old Bridget Cannon was taken from Carrick on-Shannon workhouse in Co. Leitrim and sent on a journey to the other side of the world.

Almost 160 years later, on the night of May 4th 2013, her great-great-granddaughter Neisha Wratten, who had travelled from her home in Adelaide, Australia, stepped through the doors of the same workhouse and thought about Bridget and all those who had lived and died in that building.

An estimated 4,000 Irish teenage girls, known as 'the Earl Grey girls', were sent to Australia in the late 1840's to address labour shortages and a severe gender imbalance which had evolved due to the deportation of male convicts to the British colony.

One of these was Bridget Cannon. She was first brought by horse and cart to Mullingar workhouse and from there to Dublin and on to Plymouth, where she boarded the *Lady Peel* and arrived — 110 days later — on July 3rd 1849 in Sydney.

Neisha Wratten, a gynaecologist based in Adelaide, came to Leitrim in the year of *The Gathering* to chase her ancestor's ghost.

Neisha was one of a dozen people who took part in the Famine Attic Experience, a 'living history' event organised by the Carrick-on-Shannon Historical Society as part of *The Gathering / Carrick 400* programme. The participants spent the night sleeping on a bed of straw on bare floorboards in the attic of the former workhouse, now St Patrick's Hospital, where the eerie silence and the bare whitewashed walls made her wonder about the lives of the former inmates.

An estimated 900 people, many of them children, are buried in unmarked graves at the back of the workhouse, where a Famine Garden of Remembrance has been created.

As Neisha walked slowly up Summerhill in Carrick-on-Shannon – known in the 1800's as Gallows Hill, for obvious reasons – towards the grey stone workhouse building, she wondered about Bridget's family and whether her mother, Biddy, or any of her siblings had made it into the workhouse.

"When I first entered the attic, I felt an almost palpable sense of cold and sorrow," said Neisha. "Looking out of the window, I could imagine Bridget making the long trek up to the workhouse, feeling pain in her stomach from both hunger and dread of the place. I could also see her in Mr Sweeney's cart, with her wooden box and all her possessions, going back down the hill to the Dublin Road and on to Mullingar."

Carrick-on-Shannon Historical Society has unearthed many documents from the Famine times. These include harrowing accounts by two Quaker visitors to the town in 1846, a time when hunger and disease was claiming 12 inmates every week. Conditions in the workhouse were appalling. There was no sanitation. Disease was rife and families were separated, with different quarters for men, women and children. Destitute people pleaded for sanctuary at the gates.

"There are reports that mothers with five or six children pleaded for even one or two of them to be taken in," said Neisha. "I wonder did Bridget's mother, Biddy, have to make that choice?"

She has discovered that there was no fairy-tale ending for her great-great-grandmother. Having spent 47 days in a holding depot in Sydney, she was indentured to a man called Michael O'Brien, but ran away to the convict colony of Morton Bay after just two weeks. "Something must have driven her away. We can only speculate," said Neisha.

Bridget was still 16 when she married Dublin-born John Smith, described in documents as a 'bullock driver'. Neisha has unearthed a newspaper clipping suggesting that the marriage was not a happy one. In 1891, when she was in her 50's, Bridget went to court to have her husband bound to the peace after he threatened to stick a pitchfork into her and some of her sons. Smith slept with the pitchfork under the bed and a gun under his mattress. Bridget was so terrified she slept out in the fields, according to the court report.

Neisha believes that Bridget had 14 or 15 children. One of them, Katie – her great-grandmother – died young after her skirt went on fire in a domestic accident, leaving four young children, including Neisha's grandmother, Teresa. Teresa had eight children and the youngest, Desmond, was Neisha's father.

Neisha Wratten enters the former workhouse where her great-great-grandmother, Bridget Cannon, was an inmate during the Famine.

Photograph: Brian Farrell

During the night she spent in the former workhouse in Carrick-on-Shannon, Neisha thought about Bridget and her life. "Looking up at the ceiling, I thought of the different ceilings she must have lain awake looking at in her life – the thatch of her father's croft, with holes, and smelling of smoke and animals and other humans; the vaulted roof and beams of the workhouse that must have seemed so severe and strange; the claustrophobic roof of the ship's cabin that creaked and leaked so that she must have wondered whether she would drown; and the tin roof of the house of rough gum planks that she and John lived in, and where her children were born."

Neisha's experience has made her feel close to her great-great-grandmother. "Yes, I think I did really find Bridget there. I am sure there are a lot of souls still wandering around that attic," she remarked. She is very proud of her ancestor. "I think she was a survivor. I do wonder how she would feel about this. I know people used to be ashamed about being in the workhouse, but I think Bridget was strong, and I think she would say 'tell the story'."

John Bredin, chairman of Carrick-on-Shannon Historical Society, says that it is important to remember those who lived and died in the workhouse. "And to remember that today there are still people experiencing famine in other parts of the world."

But does she feel angry about what happened to Bridget? "I feel sorry that she lived through such difficult times. I am sorry she experienced the workhouse and I am sorry she was taken from her family and sent to a strange land. I'm sorry she met a man who did not treat her well. But I am glad she made the journey – because if she did not, I would not be here. And I would like to know what she would think about her great-great-grand-daughter coming to Ireland. I hope she would be proud," Neisha replied.

Neisha discovered on her visit to Leitrim that Bridget's sister, Margaret, was baptised in Croghan Church, near Carrick-on-Shannon.

Coming to Leitrim has been, she said, very much about coming home. "I love the countryside, I love the river. I love the people. As I travelled around, and stood in the little graveyard in Croghan, I felt something very strange. I felt as if I knew the place previously. I feel at home here. It is lovely to be home."

Marese McDonagh is a freelance journalist based in the North West.

GATHERINGS
A reflection by Fergal Keane

Fergal Keane is an acclaimed journalist and Special Correspondent with the BBC.

Home is many places and feelings. It is London where I live with my wife and children. It is a part of Africa that I feel forever bound to, and a few other places around the world where I have lived intensely. And it is in Ireland where I am rooted and feel unbreakable emotional connections.

I lived in Dublin until I was 11. Then came a traumatic migration to Cork where I spent my teenage years. After that I moved to Limerick, then back to Dublin and on to Belfast, until I left Ireland in the last decade of the old century. My peripatetic life in Ireland prepared me well for a career roaming the world.

From an early age I was attuned to the possibility of sudden departures. I came of restless people. Both of my parents constantly spoke of places and ideas beyond our horizons. My father had taken the boat for London as a young man; my mother hitch-hiked around Europe at the age of 18, a great adventure for a young Irish woman in the 1950's. If at times there was a desperation spurring that restlessness, it was compensated for by a sense of the world's limitless possibilities.

I left Ireland to live in South Africa in 1990, and in the same year purchased a small cottage in Ardmore in Co. Waterford, about 45 miles east of Cork near the mouth of the River Blackwater. This is my summer 'gathering' place. It is a tin and wood structure, built in the 1930's and still – just about – weathering the storms of the Irish winter. The principal claim to fame of this little house is that Fred Astaire once stayed there. I have yet to discover why he came to so humble a dwelling.

9

I come to Ardmore every August, as I have done since I was a few months old and being 'minded' for the summer by my maternal grandmother, May Hassett. She gave us the freedom to ramble, to lose and find ourselves across the cliffs, coves and beaches as part of a large gang of children drawn from as near as Whiting Bay (one mile) and as far away as Co. Antrim. A local told me recently that we summer visitors were known as 'the swallows' to him and his friends, like those lines of Yeats:

They came like swallows and like swallows went,
And yet a woman's powerful character
Could keep a swallow to its first intent;
(Coole Park, 1929)

These days on my journeys home the destination is defined by the season. Summer is Ardmore. Christmas and the New Year will find me travelling between Cork and Ennis, dividing the days between my own family and the in-laws, motoring tentatively along icebound roads like so many other seasonal returnees, drowning in tea and catching up on news with old friends. So many of my close friends in Ireland are people I have known since I was a child. No place delights me more than Cork's English Market in the last days before Christmas, perusing the turkeys and spiced beef before having lunch in the Farm Gate.

Then it is up the road to Ennis and a New Year's Eve party with guitars and good voices. My wife Anne comes from a family of dancers and musicians. I vividly recall one of our first dates, when I wandered by mistake into a spirited – is it ever anything else? – bout of *The Siege of Ennis*. As the dancers thundered toward me across the floor I feared briefly for my safety, like a small animal that trespasses into the path of migrating wildebeest on the African savannah. Only my wife's last-minute intervention – a sturdy hand whirling me away by the waist – prevented dire injury.

Several times a year I will come back to go to rugby matches. I am a Munster fanatic and a strong Ireland supporter. Despite what some Leinster fans will tell you, the two are not mutually exclusive! I love Dublin on days when there is a big game. There is a sense of fun and warmth you won't find anywhere else in the capitals of the Six Nations.

For a long time after my parents separated and I had moved with my mother to Cork, I regarded Dublin as a city of ghosts. It was melancholy, shaded with unhappy memories, a place I wanted to avoid. Working there in the 1980's changed that. I re-discovered the city of my childhood and discovered that it held happy memories too: going to the children's cinema with my father on Grafton Street on Saturday mornings; one endless July when my mother took us swimming at Sandycove day after day; fishing at Bull Island in the autumn.

The love of Ireland has been inherited by my children Daniel and Holly. I brought Daniel to watch Ireland play France at Lansdowne Road, and he told me later that he wanted to come back and go to college in Dublin. "It's big enough and small enough, if you know what I mean," he said. I think I did.

(Opposite)
Whiting Bay, Ardmore,
Co. Waterford.

Photograph: Fergal Keane

Hot air balloons in the sky over Lough Key Forest Park during the "Return of The Rossies" gathering event.

Photograph: Brian Farrell

13

Photograph: Toru Tazura

Photographs: Alan Betson / The Irish Times

THE BALLYMALOE LITERARY FESTIVAL OF FOOD AND WINE
Rory O'Connell

Food has played a huge part in our family, and we were thrilled at Ballymaloe to host a dazzling array of talent from the world of food and drink for a special gathering this year. The idea to have a literary festival of food and wine came from a friend who runs a similar festival in Galle in Sri Lanka, and it seemed a perfect fit, in the year of *The Gathering*, for a place synonymous with the serving, teaching, talking and indeed writing about food.

Well, gather they did, and the guests walked, cycled, drove, took trains, boats and planes to get to this little corner of Ireland in the lush agricultural area of east Cork, within view of the ocean.

A group of 50 authors and speakers, both national and international, came to the event, rivalling any gathering of cooks and wine buffs ever assembled in this country. All were drawn to the place where, 50 years before, Myrtle Allen quietly opened her door to the public to serve the food she was proud of from her garden, farm and locality. Little could Mrs Allen have known that half a century later, Ballymaloe would become the centre of the world for lovers of food and wine and the words that are written on the subject.

Stephanie Alexander came all the way from Australia; Madhur Jaffrey and David Tanis came from New York; Claudia Roden, Jancis Robinson, Skye Gyngell and Thomasina Miers came from London; Claus Meyer came from *Noma* in Copenhagen; Bill Yosses came from the White House in Washington; and David Thompson came from Bangkok. Ireland was represented by chefs, food writers and critics, including Nevin Maguire, Donal Skehan, Rachel Allen, Denis Cotter, John McKenna, Tom Doorley, Mary Dowey and many more.

(Opposite above)
'The Wild and the Cultivated' workshop and Ballymaloe garden walk with Alys Fowler.

(Opposite below)
Chefs, writers and journalists gather at the Ballymaloe Literary Festival of Food and Wine.

Photographs: Joleen Cronin

Over three sunny days this group spoke, listened, debated, cooked, foraged, ate, drank, chatted and wandered – all in an atmosphere that was as charmed as it was relaxed.

The speakers were joined by about 8,000 people who came to hear their food heroes. For many, previous contact with their favourite authors had been via the printed page. Now they had the opportunity for face-to-face and voice-to-voice contact. The inked word became the spoken word. For all of us involved in this event, this was the great thrill.

There was business to be done, and many topics were discussed. The evolution of food writing was explored and old recipe books were pored over. Bloggers and self-publishing authors had their forum, as did food journalists, who had plenty of timely issues to debate. Food revolutions past, present and future were a hot topic. The intensity of these discussions permeated the entire event.

Outside of the scheduled literary events and cookery demonstrations, there was another festival going on in 'The Big Shed'. This was an open-door barn, jam-packed with a happy tangle of people of all ages. The entrance arch was woven from willow and teasels, and chandeliers made from recycled whiskey barrels hung from the rafters. Books floated in the air on invisible lines, looking like upside-down seagulls. The walls were decorated with drawings of handsome chickens and country life from the primary school in Shanagarry, and the weekend's resident graffiti artist filled in any gaps. The eclectic beauty of the setting was matched by the beautiful noise that was created: the clink of glasses, the sizzle of grills, the crunch of knives being drawn through crusty bread, the whistle of kettles boiled for a cup of tea, the intoxicating sound of laughter and chat.

Gardeners rubbed shoulders with cooks, foragers with food historians, critics with musicians, artisan producers with bloggers, seed savers with book sellers, and authors with readers. This was an area for free speech and pop-up forums – a melting pot of words read, spoken, remembered, recited, sung or hummed. There was no pecking order, no formality. While you quenched your thirst on a local craft beer or cider, and satisfied your hunger on a sandwich of chorizo from west Cork or a slice of warm roast local chicken, you were as likely to be sitting alongside an iconic food writer as you were your neighbour.

The famous were disarmed, the anonymous were recognised. All were welcomed.

Rory O'Connell is a chef and teacher at the world-renowned Ballymaloe Cookery School, and the brother of Darina Allen.

(Left)
*Enthusiastic participants at
the Ballymaloe Literary
Festival of Food and Wine.*

(Left middle)
Afternoon tea with Myrtle Allen.

(Left bottom)
*Take three past students …
Rachel Allen, Thomasina Miers
and Stevie Parle
conducting a cookery
demonstration.*

(Below)
*Young foodies taking part in Big
Shed Fringe Festival at the
Ballymaloe Literary Festival of
Food and Wine.*

Photographs: Joleen Cronin

THE RHYTHM OF LIFE
A reflection by Moya Doherty

Moya Doherty is a co-founder and producer of the world acclaimed Riverdance.

It was always a bit of a puzzle to me, this 'being Irish' thing. I never really knew what it meant. If you grew up in a border town in the 1950's and 1960's, as I did, you had a particular lilt to your language and a particular list to your thinking.

Pettigo, Co. Donegal. The main street: Britton's pub, the Custom House.

Ms Bishop, the Protestant music teacher. The local primary school. Mr and Mrs Snow across the road who sold their religious artefacts in a stall on the shores of Lough Derg. The Tamlaght road with the milk churns. The post office at the top of the town where my mother bought me my first green, white and gold apron to help with the house-work. Dust under the beds, lino on the floor, a hand-rotated dryer, the well at the end of the garden, the chipped crockery set for the Crolly doll's dinner.

Reid's sweet shop, a skip and a hop away from our rented lodgings. The old, red leatherette-seated, yellow Volkswagen Beetle. The Silver Cross pram where the next baby sat, strapped in under the milky spring sunshine. The Cardinal Red polished front step.

The rhythm of life in a border town. Once a border town girl, forever on the border. The border of life.

The trips to Enniskillen — the first one home from the Erne hospital, the third girl of the two school teachers. The clattering noise as I wore my mother's white, patent leather, high heels, clip-clopping along the Ballyshannon hospital floor, visiting the next newborn sibling.

(Opposite)
Illustration by Mark McColgan (23) Rhode Island School of Design, US.

The sweet sound of the Irish language. The rhythm of the walk, the rhythm of the talk.

Across the bog, much further west in the county, Granny on the doorstep, fleshy arms folded – skin the gloss of aluminum foil; thick-tongued, broken English spoken.

Uncle Connie in the shoe shop selling only the farm work-boot or the black wellington or the sturdy brogues for the country woman. No truck with style. Brown paper and string, the boxes of leather-smelling Clarks shoes stacked high, the Irish Press cross-word, the black and white television with the rabbit ears, the hatch into the kitchen to hear Granny call her bachelor son to dinner at one o'clock.

The rhythm of leaving. The rhythm of losing.

The Sunday trips to Cloghboile to grand-uncle Dan. A *streally* countryman who never left the house he was born into. Gable end to the sea, front facing the road. The Sunday cooking steaming from the range in Granny's kitchen. Soda bread wrapped in a tea towel, bacon and cabbage, spuds, sweet apple pie, parsnips and carrots. A mackerel. A week's sustenance for Dan the stammerer, Dan the loner, Dan the bachelor. Dan, whose brothers and sisters – all but Granny Bridget – headed north to Scotland, east to London, Chichester and beyond.

Across the street from Mulhern's Corner Bar in Dungloe, the Doherty clan, returned immigrants. Back from the Depression in New York to run a small business and rear a family, leaving behind the many sisters and brothers to settle forever in the Bronx, Brooklyn and beyond. The rhythm of the home place beckoned.

The first journey at seven years of age from Donegal to Dublin.

The melting into a big city. That first bus ride to the heart of the city: Nelson's pillar, Clerys' Clock, Guineys, McBirney's, MacLiammóir in the Gate, McAnally in the Abbey. Poetry in the classroom, music lessons, this time from Mrs Kelly across the road in Dollymount Avenue, feeding her furry little poodle biscuits as the crumbs fell down on my teenage fingers.

The Belgrove National School teacher painting her toenails shocking pink under the desk. The Aran sweater knitted by my sister Nuala, so complex and intricate she was made explain each stitch to the class at age ten to ensure intellectual property. Ms O'Reagan and her love of language and dance. The embarrassing strip-down to the grey-white vest and knickers to be weighed by the school nurse, bellowing out my eight stone weight, shamed, as all the other girls barely registered six stone on the scales.

The clatter and clump of the long and the short and the tall of us hammering on the school hall floor at the Irish dance class. *A haon, dó, trí, ceathair, cúig, sé, seacht … is a haon, dó, trí … is a haon, dó, trí …*

The rhythm of a journey. The rhythm of the everyday.

The Manor House School in Raheny: nuns whose memory might just give nuns a good name. Sr Alacoque, not cut out for the habit – but a wizard of a basketball coach. Sr Theresa, the tsetse fly who shocked the innocent, asserting that all natural disasters were a means of stabilising the world population. Sr Ephrem – the little effer – tiny and fearful of her wards. Mrs Parker and her passionate love of theatre. Ms Barrow and her passionate love of music.

May processions around the basketball courts. The remnants of the first communion garb, worn, pressed together with pins.

The rhythmical shift to the world of a young adult.

The basement of North Great George's Street, rehearsing Shakespeare's plays. The bus journeys, touring the towns of Ireland with Sundrive Players on the amateur drama circuit. Best Supporting Actress award, somewhere.

Another decade into the 1980's, the divorce referendum rejected, the abortion referendum rejected, the strut of the Fianna Fáil politicians as they'd preen all around in their attempt to control RTE.

From secretary to TV presenter, then on to the boat to London in search of another border.

The rhythm of departure. The rhythm of the immigrant.

London in the Thatcher years, the bombing of Harrods, and the shame of being told, when I spelt out loud my northern nationalist name, that 'h' was pronounced 'aitch' and not 'haitch'.

Five years of cosmopolitan colour – a thousand years away from the border town. Learning to shape the Irishness in the emerging frame of a woman built from memories of the past. The gentle London neighbours, Charlie and Sally, settled a lifetime in Islington, burning turf and growing shamrock.

The locals from Africa, India, the Caribbean, Ireland, gathering in Donegal Charlie's corner off-licence, settling on orange boxes, clambering their way through the politics of the day.

The rhythm of return. The ultimate yearning to head back to a place called home.

The love of a good man. The decision to marry.

The joy of the return.

The birth of two healthy sons.

The emerging rhythm of life, the beat of the drum of time, the search for a voice. The rhythm of an idea in the corridors of RTE. The rhythm of opportunity. The meeting of minds that shaped the music and the dance. The explosion of Irishness, a new rhythm to the roots.

The opening nights. Dublin, London, New York, Sydney, Japan, Beijing. The standing ovations.

The rhythm of the music. The rhythm of the dance. The rhythm of Irishness.

It was always a bit of a puzzle to me, this 'being Irish' thing.

Members of the Riverdance cast who were part of the 1,693 dancers who broke the world record for the longest Riverdance line as part of the Riverdance Gathering weekend in July 2013.

Photograph:
Alan Betson / The Irish Times

IRISH COMMUNITY CARE, MANCHESTER
Fiona McGarry

Hailstones, chill winds and driving rain did nothing to dampen the spirits of the 62 men and women from Manchester Irish Community Care who travelled to the west of Ireland for a very special gathering.

Most of the group – ten of whom were over the age of 80 – were first-generation Irish who had emigrated to the north of England in the 1950's and 1960's. Well used to the unpredictability of the Irish weather, they were determined to make the most of their week-long trip to Mayo. "We had a different experience every day, and that's not just in terms of weather," laughed Cath Cunningham, Volunteer Coordinator with the organisation, which caters mainly to the elderly among the Irish community in Manchester. "I even managed to get sunburned in Castlebar, despite the showers!"

Back in Manchester, Cath coordinates a team of 50 volunteers who work with the Irish community to alleviate poverty, loneliness and distress in old age. This is done through a range of projects which provide advice and support, as well as social contact and companionship. The decision to travel to Ireland during the year of *The Gathering* was prompted partly by the group's existing programme of excursions and outings. "Last year alone, we had eight different day-trips," explained Cath. "Then, two of our more senior ladies said, 'Never mind going to Blackpool to look at the lights, why can't we go to Ireland?' I asked where they would go, and they immediately said, 'Knock' ".

"Religion is still very strong with a lot of our members," Cath noted. "They wanted the most holy places in Ireland, so we chose Knock, Croagh Patrick and Ballintubber Abbey."

Irish Community Care helpers Sylvia Spilling, Nancy Devine and Cath Cunningham.

Photograph: Tony Hennigan

But there was plenty of time, over the course of the visit, for other pursuits. Heritage and history were enjoyed at Foxford Woollen Mills, as well as a civic reception at the National Museum of Ireland - Country Life in Turlough. There were hours of shopping in Castlebar with the deputy mayor thanking the group for their contribution to the economy!

The importance of *The Gathering* year in economic terms was not lost on others taking part in the trip. Monica Sloyan (neé O'Grady) is a Community Care volunteer originally from Kiltimagh in east Mayo. She was saddened by the impact of the downturn on her native town. "It's a different Kiltimagh nowadays," she observed. "It's sad to see so many places closed down. There was a great buzz of life about the town, but it seems so quiet now. We're glad to be able to bring in some business, even if that's just for a week."

In addition to enjoying the amenities of the county, many of the group were able to share their memories of home. For Monica, being able to point out the house where she grew up on James Street in Kiltimagh was among the emotional highlights of the visit. For others, coming back to Ireland brought mixed feelings. "We went to Foxford, and one of the ladies hadn't been back there since she was 14," Cath explained. "She saw the church she was christened in. It was really, really touching."

As Cath and the other volunteers understand, emigration is a complex issue. Travelling home in a group means everyone receives the support they might need. "It's not always easy for people to come back," she noted. "People leave for different reasons. Coming as a group means there's no pressure on people to go and stay with family, where there may have been conflict in the past. We've had a lot of people meet their family here [at the hotel] and that's worked well." Renewing her own family connections on Achill Island was a highlight for Cath.

To celebrate *Bealtaine*, the annual festival of creativity in older age, the group joined with St Colman's Day Care Centre in Keel for a tea dance with a difference. The visitors were greeted in traditional style by one of Achill's acclaimed pipers, John McNamara. Monica, like many others, found it an unforgettable island welcome. "Being piped in off the coach was very emotional. We were made to feel so welcome. I couldn't help thinking, 'Will I ever come back again?'."

"We wanted the group to have the best visit possible," Cath said. "I was crying like a baby when I saw the piper. Traditionally, a piper signifies a big occasion like a wedding or a funeral. It was so emotional. The sad fact is that for one or two of our group, it will be their last trip home ever."

The tea dance was also an occasion for reminiscences and happy coincidences. The group were amazed to meet singer-songwriter Gerry Carney, writer of the poignant *Paddy,* a ballad about an emigrant Irishman living in Manchester. "Gerry had heard about the tea dances because his wife is from Achill," Cath explained. "He had no idea we were going to be there. The song *Paddy* is about men that Gerry met in Levenshulme, where half of our ladies live. When he explained that, he got a massive response."

Achill itself is also full of echoes of the emigrant experience. The island has seen decades of emigration – much of it seasonal, to service the potato-growing industry in Scotland. Cath's grandmother was one of those 'tattie hokers'.

"It was a very hard life," Cath noted. "My granny lost a hand in a fire, so her job was to be house-keeper for those who went out to work in the potato fields. Emigrants from Ireland have suffered greatly through the generations, and we're very aware of that."

Monica too remembers tougher times for the Irish abroad. Her husband Aidan, who first emigrated in the 1950's, saw the harsher side of life. "He used to tell me about the signs saying, *No dogs or Irish allowed*. I didn't find that. I found people very welcoming, but I know it wasn't like that for everyone."

In recognition of generations gone before, a visit to the National Famine Memorial at Murrisk was also on the itinerary. "We had to see that," Cath said. "It was about paying tribute to people who have gone before, and acknowledging how lucky we are. There were so many who left, who never got to come back home."

And, as this particular gathering drew to a close, the question on everyone's lips was, 'When are we coming back?' "Everyone's already asking," laughed Cath. "This trip was incredible. The welcome we've had in Mayo has been overwhelming. Everyone will take away such great memories, and who knows what's in store for 2014?"

Fiona McGarry is a freelance broadcaster and journalist. She also teaches journalism at the University of Limerick.

Photographs:
Malcolm McGettigan/
BigOMedia

*Members of the No. 3 Gun Attachment during a Ceremonial
21 Gun Salute by the First Southern Brigade Army on Spike Island on
New Year's Day, to mark the start of The Gathering.*

Photograph: Michael MacSweeney / Provision

A CROSS-BORDER BODY
A reflection by Mrs Justice Catherine McGuinness

Mrs Justice Catherine McGuinness is a retired Supreme Court Judge, former Senator and activist.

When I was invited to contribute to this book it was suggested to me that I might reflect on the concept of Irishness in the light of the changes that have taken place "since you came to live here". Of course I have to start by asserting that I have always lived in Ireland – I was born in Belfast, which is now generally acknowledged to be part of that useful entity, 'the island of Ireland'. I therefore have no difficulty in believing that I can be part of the concept of Irishness.

Following my primary education I came to live at least part time in Dublin as a boarder in Clergy Daughters' School. Through my third-level education in Trinity College Dublin and through all my adult life, I have remained resident in Dublin, while retaining a pride in my birthplace and many continuing connections north of the border. During the peace process much emphasis was laid on the evolution of 'cross-border bodies'. With a father from west Clare, a mother from Tullamore, and a birthplace in Belfast, I think that I have a good claim to be an actual cross-border body myself, and I often made this claim when I was Chair of the Forum for Peace and Reconciliation in the early stages of the peace process.

Nevertheless, it is true that the social, religious and political life in Dublin was a strange enough world for a Northern Protestant teenager in the 1950's. On all sides it was made clear, both by inference and overtly, that to be truly Irish was to be Catholic, Irish-

HARPER FAMILY REUNION
Jill Harper

When Sergeant Robert Harper was posted to Kilkenny in the early 1800's, he hardly imagined that just shy of 200 years later, 274 of his descendants would gather in Kilkenny to celebrate the Harper family.

Robert had watched all (bar one) of his sons leave for Canada. One wonders what he would have thought on seeing 81 out of those 274 descendants returning from 11 different countries, from as far apart as Hong Kong and Sweden, Hawaii and Zimbabwe.

Inspired by *The Gathering*, the push was on to make the fourth Harper Reunion extra special. In fact, since the last one in 2006, the family had seen 70 births and 14 marriages. The attendance at the 2013 reunion was a third larger again than the previous one.

Kilkenny College proved a fantastic venue for this fun-filled event, as classrooms became art galleries and the study hall a hive of activity. The reunion's theme of creativity saw a psalm written and performed at the talent show, ad hoc Irish dancing at a *céilí*, and a collaborative piece of art created from everyone's individual fingerprint. All ages were catered for, with generational games, an interactive children's programme and seminars for the adults. The weekend featured memorable visits to James Stephens Barracks, where Sergeant Robert had served, and to the original home place; as well as an excursion to Nore Valley Park.

The event was streamed live online, with Skype calls enabling those who couldn't attend to participate from afar. The youngest member of the family, Ian, at only two

(Opposite)
The Harper family enjoying their reunion.

(Top left)
Photograph: Dale Harper

(Top right and bottom)
Photographs: Keith Dowling

weeks old, greeted his extended family from Perth, Australia. At 96 years of age, Bill Harper had time to share memories with his 94-year-old cousin, Robin Harper, who had travelled all the way from Pennsylvania. Old connections were rekindled and new friendships forged, as the intimacy of family was restored for a new generation.

A great effort was made by the organising team to collect and preserve the stories, memories and wisdom of an ageing generation. It was no small feat for the photographer who had the unenviable task of taking the group picture – imagine trying to get 274 people to say 'cheese' together! Indeed, photos were an important feature over the weekend, as new snaps were taken and old ones shared.

Sunday morning was an ecumenical experience, as the wide breadth of Christian expression within the family came together. There was music from contemporary to traditional hymns; praying Pentecostals to enthusiastic Evangelicals; an open communion and a sermon on the importance of family in the Christian tradition. It was a very appropriate closing ceremony that encouraged and inspired everyone present.

(Above)
274 Harpers.

Photograph: Keith Dowling

(Right)
"Eight is Enough?"
Pictured are Leslie and June Harper of Bandon, Cork with their eight grandchildren, at the Harper Family Reunion.

Photograph: June Harper

SOMETIMES YOU CAN'T MAKE IT ON YOUR OWN

A reflection by Bono

Sometimes you can't make it on your own
tough, you think you've got the stuff
you're telling me and anyone
you're hard enough
you don't have to put up a fight
you don't have to always be right
let me take some of the punches
for you tonight

listen to me now
I need to let you know
you don't have to go it alone

and its you when I look in the mirror
and its you when I don't pick up the phone
Sometimes you can't make it on your own

we fight...
all the time....
you and I...
thats alright
we're the same soul

I dont need
I dont need to hear you say
that if we weren't so alike
you'd like me a whole lot more

The lead singer of U2, Bono was born in Dublin.

Illustration and hand-written lyrics by Bono

listen to me now
I need to let you know
you dont have to go it alone

and its you when I look in the mirror
and its you when I dont pick up the phone
Sometimes you cant make it on your own

I know that we dont talk
Im sick of it all
but can you hear me when I sing?
you're the reason I sing
you're the reason why the opera is in me
Hey now   still got to let you know
a house does not make a home
Dont leave me here ALONE !
and its you when I look in the mirror
and its you that makes it hard to let go
Sometimes you cant make it on your own
sometimes you cant make it
best you can do is to fake it
Sometimes you cant make it on your own.

Bono 4 IRISH HOSPICE FOUNDATION · 2013

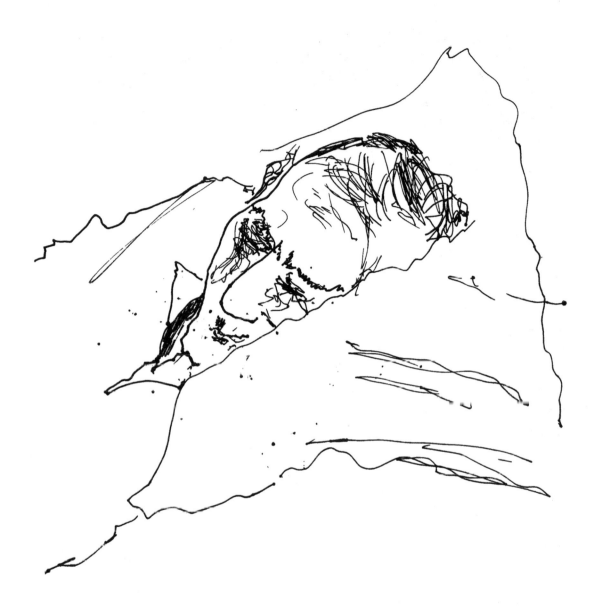

Sleepinsidethepilla 11.25 20,18 00.

Detail from 'Sleep Inside the Pillow'
illustration of Bob Hewson by Bono.

In character are Séamus Harlowe and Saoirse Walsh.

Photograph: Andrew Downes

THE SHANTALLA GATHERING
Dave O'Connell

When it comes to unique get-togethers in the year of *The Gathering*, the sight of the President of Ireland, Michael D Higgins, sipping afternoon tea with Daniel O'Connell himself, in the shadow of Shantalla's famous Sliding Rock, would take some beating. Just what the two great orators — separated by a century-and-a-half — might have discussed is anyone's guess, but the chances are that the community spirit of Galway's oldest housing estate might be well up the list.

Shantalla, on the west side of the city, turned 70 years old in 2013 and like any local authority estate in the country, it has known its share of good times and bad. But it retains a sense of its own identity that makes you wonder why they didn't have a community festival before now. It could be that Galway breeds festivals as the Coolmore Stud breeds Group One winners — celebrating horseracing and oysters, arts and film, sailing and seafood, poetry and children. The good people of Shantalla may have felt that there was no room for another.

But *Seachtain an tSeanthalamh* (Shantalla Week) was a community festival in the best sense of the word, with no big names (unless you include the President back on home ground, and Daniel O'Connell, of course) and no big budget — just friends and neighbours gathering to welcome others back.

Seventy must be the magic number in Shantalla. It started off in 1943 with the first 70 houses, and every family who ever lived there is chronicled in a new book that charts

the human history of this integral part of Galway. It has expanded, of course, over the years, and it now boasts almost 400 houses and around 3,000 inhabitants – but it has never lost that sense of community, of belonging. Tony Flannery, who produced the book, remembers his own family moving there from the Claddagh, into one of the earliest three-bedroom houses on O'Conaire Road. They had just one light in the kitchen and one plug at the fireplace. There was no bathroom, just a tiny upstairs toilet.

As for me, my mother was one of the Hunts from Shantalla; my father's eldest brother, Bernie, was a stalwart of the community there, and, by extension, I claim a slice of my own heritage in this bastion of old Galway.

Seachtain an tSeanthalamh and the linked Shantalla gathering coincided with the 70th anniversary, with expats home from Boston, London and Australia for the celebrations. This was about 12 events: 'The Streets of Shantalla' with the best athletes from each of the area's 12 roads – Ash Road, Carrick Road, Coleman's Road, Colmcille Road, Costello Road, Davis Road, Enda's Road, Fursey Road, McDara Road, O'Conaire Road, O'Flaherty Road, Reddington Road – competing for the glory alone.

Five-a-side soccer, a family fun day, nightly music, a banquet, a photo exhibition – it might not have been the Cannes Film Festival, but it was real and authentic, and it was down to people like John Anthony McDonagh, chairman of Shantalla Community Association, and Tom Nally, PRO, who made it all happen on a shoestring.

The re-enactment of Daniel O'Connell's address from the Sliding Rock in 1843, organised by Peter Connolly, Ann Butler and Alice O'Sullivan, was a perfect centrepiece to the week. The Sliding Rock, as it is known to one and all, is at the heart of Shantalla – a massive stone mound with a stone cross on top, where O'Connell gathered the faithful in his quest to repeal the Act of Union. It is a spot that is very dear to generations who had more mundane uses for its steep slopes, such as sliding from its peak.

One presumes O'Connell didn't have the luxury of a specially erected canopy, but the atmosphere was evocative and electric as actor, Séamus Ó hAodha – veteran of TV programmes, *Ros na Rún* and *Rásaí na Gaillimhe* – delivered the great man's rabble-rousing words with an authority that the legendary man of Cahirsiveen would have been proud of.

The Sliding Rock oration was the highlight of the first weekend of *Seachtain an tSeanthalamh*, the seven-day celebration of the Shantalla community that had something for everyone, sports, arts, music, history, parades and a banquet.

The five-a-side soccer blitz on Saturday had its share of nostalgia when a team of relative veterans from the defunct, but temporarily reformed, Corrib Shamrocks club – a team that grew to sweep all before them back in the 1970's – got into the spirit of things by donning long wigs in memory of an era when they all had hair.

It was that type of week – there were structured events and a packed programme, but the emphasis was on making your own fun and enjoying your own community.

And Galway found out it had room for one more festival after all. What a gathering it was too!

Dave O'Connell is the Group Editor of The Connacht Tribune.

Women from St. Joseph's Ladies Club and Westside Community getting into the spirit of the Shantalla Gathering.

Photograph:
Joe O'Shaughnessy

Descendants of Irish people who fled for Canada during the Great Famine, Frances Kilbride (89) and Richard Tye (76) meet for the first time at the Irish National Famine Museum at Strokestown Park, Co. Roscommon.

Photograph: Brian Farrell

Children recreating happy memories during a gathering to celebrate the Centenary of the Iveagh Trust Play Centre in Dublin which was known as the Bayno. Thousands of children attended the Bayno after school to partake in education, fun and games between 1913 and the 1970's.

Photograph: Alan Betson / The Irish Times

As part of the Spirit of Connemara event, hundreds of US visitors at Shannon Airport were surprised with dawn dancing by Sean-Nós sensation Emma O'Sullivan and music from the Mulkerrins Brothers from the Aran Islands.

Photograph: Sean Curtin

A LEGACY TO BUILD UPON

A reflection by Tom Arnold

Tom Arnold is a former CEO of the Irish aid agency, Concern Worldwide.

The Irish have a 'wandering' gene somewhere in their genetic code. Over the centuries people have left Ireland in search of employment, new opportunities or excitement. *The Gathering* is tapping into a variation of how this same gene expresses itself: the desire to come home, at least for a time.

Early in 2013 I stepped down as CEO of Concern Worldwide, having served in the role for over 11 years. In that position I had the privilege of meeting with a large number of modern-day Irish wanderers, whether as missionaries, employees of NGOs or businesspeople. Wherever I met them, in Africa, Asia or Haiti, I was struck by the contribution they were making to their adopted countries.

Many of our Irish missionaries are now in the closing years of their work. We will never see their like again. It is important that this generation of Irish people acknowledges the huge and valuable contribution they have made.

Our missionaries have contributed over many different fields, including health, agriculture, education and community development. The late Dr Daniel Murphy of Trinity College, Dublin, has contended, in his magisterial study, *A History of Irish Emigrant and Missionary Education*, published in 2000, that, "Far and away the most valuable contribution made by Irish immigrants to the society in which they settled has been in the sphere of education. They provided education of the highest standard on five continents – Europe, America, Africa, Asia, and Australia – contributing to the development of their own expatriate fellow countrymen and to the indigenous peoples in the countries where they settled."

Dr Murphy situates his argument and his evidence, the product of a lifetime of scholarship, over the sweep of centuries. The process began in the 6th century, with the exodus of Irish monastic educators to Europe, where, over the following six centuries, they made a lasting contribution to monastic culture and learning across the continent.

It resumed with the founding of the Irish colleges in various parts of Europe in the 16th century, a movement that involved large numbers of Irish teachers and students, and which expanded eventually to more than 30 colleges.

A far greater exodus of Irish educators began with the great migrations to North America in the 17th century. This reached flood-like proportions in the 19th century (especially post-Famine), resulting in the creation by Irish migrants of distinctive systems of education in the US and Canada.

The whole process reached its peak in the missionary movement in Africa and Asia from the late 19th century, a movement which was overwhelmingly educational in character and concerned directly with the provision of schools for the peoples of these regions.

In their own way, modern Irish NGOs fit into this great tradition, even if none have any evangelical role. The three largest Irish NGOs operating internationally – Concern Worldwide, Trócaire and Goal – are recognised as being effective, professional and committed, while a number of smaller NGOs are making their own distinctive contribution. Even the timing of the establishment of Concern (1968), Trócaire (1973) and Goal (1977) might be interpreted as a passing of the baton from a missionary tradition to a new organisational form, but which, in the case of both missionaries and NGOs, has facilitated a broad community of people living in Ireland to connect and show solidarity with the development of less fortunate people in poorer countries, especially in Africa.

The developing *modus operandi* of these NGO organisations over the past four decades has also reflected the process of change which occurred within the missionary movement. Thus, the indigenisation of local churches, as missionaries grew older and fewer, was reflected in the language and the workings of the NGOs as they shifted from mainly using young Irish volunteers in the 1970's and 1980's to localisation, capacity building and partnership.

The decades ahead will bring new challenges. Over the past ten years many African countries have become more politically stable and have registered impressive levels of economic growth. New communications technology and developments in the life sciences provide further opportunities. But huge challenges remain: 40% of African children under the age of five are stunted due to malnutrition; food production needs to increase rapidly to meet the needs of a population expected to double over the next 30 years, and we do not know what impact climate change may yet have.

Ireland has a deservedly proud tradition of being outward-looking and generous-spirited towards countries less well off than ourselves – even during these difficult economic times at home. *The Gathering* provided an opportunity to reflect on this very positive legacy, earned over centuries, and to begin the thinking on what might be our most appropriate and effective contribution in the decades to come.

Children with drawings of items that their families received from Concern. Masisi, North Kivu, Democratic Republic of the Congo.

Photograph: Kim Haughton

THE MORPETH ROLL
Terence Dooley

(Above)
George Howard, (Lord Morpeth),
c.1835, by Thomas Carrick from
the Castle Howard Collection.

(Opposite)
The Morpeth Roll with just
seven of its 420 metres unrolled
in the Russell Library at NUI
Maynooth.

Photographs:
Peter Smith Photography

It has been variously described as "one of Ireland's most extraordinary historic documents"; "a remarkable parting gift for an Englishman" upon leaving Ireland; "possibly the largest farewell card in existence"; and for many years, in its home at Castle Howard in Yorkshire, it was simply referred to as "the lavatory roll".

It is, in fact, a testimonial, now better known as *The Morpeth Roll*. It was organised by Daniel O'Connell and Augustus Frederick FitzGerald (1791-1874), the third Duke of Leinster, to mark the departure of George Howard (1802-64), then styled Viscount Morpeth, as Chief Secretary of Ireland in 1841. It was signed by 160,000 Irish people as a mark of respect to his popularity and in acknowledgement of his role in social and political reform in Ireland between 1836 and 1841.

It is fitting that this document, which originally involved the gathering of so many signatures, went on tour in Ireland in 2013 to mark the year of *The Gathering*.

For 170 years the testimonial had not been seen in public. For most of that period, it had been hidden away in the archives of Castle Howard in Yorkshire, one of the grandest privately-owned country houses in Britain, renowned as the setting for both the television series and the more recent film version of Evelyn Waugh's famous novel, *Brideshead Revisited*.

Its re-discovery followed a serendipitous meeting between myself and Professor Christopher Ridgway, the curator of Castle Howard, at a conference in London in

2004. The following year, Professor Ridgway came to the National University of Ireland Maynooth (NUIM) to address the Annual Historic Houses of Ireland Conference. He was introduced to Carton House, one of Ireland's finest surviving 18th century Palladian mansions, and the story of the Dukes of Leinster. The names began to resonate with him, and on his return to Castle Howard he went into the bowels of the archive to look again at a solid wooden trunk which he had been passing for years, and re-read the inscription:

The Address of the Reformers of Ireland
To Lord Viscount Morpeth
Presented by His Grace the Duke of Leinster
At the Royal Exchange in the City of Dublin
On Tuesday the 14th Sept[embe]r 1841.

It was then that the process of re-discovery began. Inside the trunk was a massive roll, 420 metres in length, comprised of 652 individual sheets of paper which had been stuck to a linen backdrop and wrapped around a bobbin, before being carefully inserted in the trunk. The testimonial – three times the length of Croke Park if rolled out, and almost the height of the Empire State Building – had been signed the length and breadth of Ireland to proclaim the "outpourings of affection and support" which the 160,000 signatories had for Lord Morpeth, who had to resign his position as Chief Secretary for Ireland following the loss of his parliamentary seat in Yorkshire in the general election of 1841.

The individual sheets of papers were then transported to Dublin, a journey greatly facilitated by the expanding coach network developed by Charles Bianconi (1786-1875), whose signature is one of the first to be found on the roll. On 14th September 1841, the testimonial was presented to Morpeth at a function at the Royal Exchange, which was followed by an extravagant banquet at the Theatre Royal. Morpeth declared that the roll would be "the richest heirloom" he could bequeath to his family. It was a significant statement, given that his family mansion was a treasure trove of decorative art and fine collections.

When the roll was re-discovered, the historical research into this very valuable Irish political document of the pre-Famine era took place at NUIM on the very campus originally donated by the second Duke of Leinster for the establishment of St Patrick's College in 1795.

In 2010, the owner of Castle Howard, Hon. Simon Howard, agreed to loan the roll to NUIM for research and conservation. The latter has been carried out to the highest standards by Paul Hoary of the Russell Library, while Dr Patrick Cosgrove, a research officer appointed by the Centre for the Study of Historic Irish Houses and Estates, rigorously investigated the provenance of the roll and the ceremonial proceedings around its presentation. In 2012, Ancestry.com digitised and indexed the roll, making it fully searchable for the first time ever.

One of the first signatories to be identified was Henry White from Booterstown in Dublin, a direct ancestor of the late Princess Diana. On hearing of this discovery, her son, the Duke of Cambridge, wrote to the president of NUIM on 4th April 2013, expressing his gratitude that this family connection had been brought to his attention. He found it extraordinary that "such a physically huge document should have remained unremarked and undiscovered for almost 150 years", and delighted in the fact that "the opportunities it now provides for research must be inestimable."

The Morpeth Roll means historians can now examine Irish society and reform politics in the pre-Famine period in a new way. As Christopher Ridgway remarked: "Quite simply, anyone is entitled to ask, 'Is my ancestor on this list?'" When, for example, Dr Ciaran Reilly looked at the signatories from his home town of Edenderry in Co. Offaly (in 1841, King's County), he found that the signing of the testimonial had been organised by the parish priest, Fr James Colgan. He also discovered that Joseph Rothery owned the quarry from which the stone was used to build the Edenderry Workhouse in 1841 and that Arthur Keating was a gunsmith on the Main Street who emigrated to Minnesota during the Famine.

Starting in March 2013 as part of *The Gathering*, the roll and accompanying exhibition embarked on an 18 month nationwide tour of Ireland, taking in Westport, Derrynane, Clonmel, Kilkenny, Belfast and Dublin, enabling the public to see it for the first time in 170 years. It is also the subject of a collection of essays edited by Christopher Ridgway and published by Four Courts Press, entitled *The Morpeth Roll, Ireland Identified in 1841*.

Terence Dooley is currently Associate Professor of History at NUIM and the Director of the Centre for the Study of Historic Irish Houses and Estates.

The bobbin removed from the chest in the Russell Library at NUI Maynooth.

Mike Foy in his vintage 1932 'Smithfield Special' which took part in a special gathering event - a Grand Prix race on the Carrigrohane Straight in Cork commemorating the 1938 Grand Prix race in the city.

Photograph:
Michael Mac Sweeney / Provision

IRELAND FROM OUTER SPACE
A reflection by Commander Chris Hadfield

Commander Chris Hadfield retired in 2013 after 35 years as a pilot and astronaut. He served as Commander of the International Space Station.

The first glimpse you get of earth after you launch in a space shuttle from the Kennedy Space Centre in Florida is the green of Ireland. It is a wonderful sight when the sun shines through the cloud and you see a green, green jewel, after all the blue of the Atlantic.

Space can be a lonely place, but it was made less lonely for me as I connected with so many Irish people during my last mission before retiring as an astronaut. Looking down from my perch in space, Ireland was just a tiny speck on the western fringes of Europe, yet it managed to have a huge impact as I orbited earth.

Everyone knows someone from Ireland. I grew up with an Irish boy in my native Canada - Seán Kennedy, one of my best friends. While I don't have my roots in Ireland, I have a strong connection, as our daughter Kristin is studying in Trinity College. On visits, we hiked in the hills, saw historic towers and drove through pretty villages. I drank my favourite beer, Guinness, in Irish bars. And I was amazed to see palm trees growing in parks in Dublin.

When I was in orbit on my last space flight I tweeted a picture. I wasn't sure if it was an Irish, Welsh or English port city, but I was quickly advised by those who saw it that it was Dublin. This sparked an instant and strong connection between me and the people of Ireland, divided as we were by over 200 miles. I found this amazing, like meeting a friend for the first time. It was a friendship that flourished and developed – a connection from space that just grew and grew.

I tweeted more pictures from Ireland during my mission: the sweeping coastline of Cork; Thunder Rock on the western edge of Ireland, with the Dingle Marina visible; and Sligo. I played *The Road to Sligo* many times with an Irish band, but this was the first time I had seen it from space.

Over the years I have played a lot of Irish, folk and Celtic music with different bands. Through music you get a feel for a region and its people. Growing up in Canada I lived on an isolated farm, and every Saturday night, on a black-and-white TV with rabbit ears, we watched a band called *The Irish Rover*, and I think that is where my passion for Irish music began.

I love the Dubliners, Van Morrison and Christy Moore. One of my favourite songs to sing is *Ride On*. In June, on my last night with NASA in Houston, Texas, before retiring, I played a Van Morrison song.

While my family are not from Ireland, I feel aligned to Ireland in spirit. I was really proud to have tweeted from space in Irish. Over the years I learned to speak a few languages – French, German and some Russian, as I worked as an astronaut in a Russian spaceship. When I started to engage with so many people from Ireland, I decided to tweet in Irish from space and got help from my son, Evan, and from a friend of my daughter, Kristin.

Sharing emotions and language with the Irish people was phenomenal. The warm gush of acceptance that I experienced on this space flight was special. People all over the world wanted me to take a picture of where they were from – but interest was strongest from Ireland. The connection became a two-way one between me and them, back and forth.

I think Irish people have a true understanding of who they are in the world. I know Ireland has been through some tough times in recent years. Kristen is doing a Ph.D. in psychology; she has been focusing on families and schools as part of her studies, and she has shared with me what is happening in the country.

A lot of young Irish people have emigrated, but it is possible to be proud and to re-member where you are from, yet still live somewhere else. I have done that in my life, as I have lived away from Canada for many years. But you can never take away that feeling of home.

As I write this, myself and my wife Helene are driving back to Canada, returning home for the next phase of our lives. We said goodbye to Houston, Texas, and to all our friends at NASA and are looking forward to returning home and to what lies ahead.

I will continue to play with my band, *Vandella*, and to play Irish music.

With the huge response I got from Irish people, I know that when I go back I will have an entire land of friends to visit. I will be able to go into a pub or knock on any door and I will be welcome. I suppose I can boast that I have a unique perspective on Ireland, seeing it and connecting with it as I did from space on my last mission.

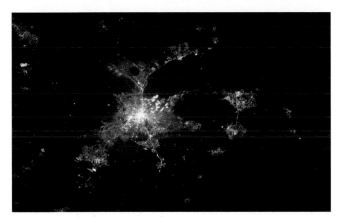 

'Tá Éire fíorálainn! Land of green and dark beer.'

Tweet in Irish sent from space by Commander Chris Hadfield

(Top left)
Big storm swirling off the Irish coast.
(Top right)
Ireland, Wales and Isle of Man silhouetted in the setting sun.
(Bottom left)
Golden lights from Dublin to Paris.
(Bottom right)
A clear Dublin night in early spring.

Photographs: Commander Chris Hadfield

BYRNE GATHERING
Wicklow

120 descendants of John and Mary Byrne came together at the Avon Rí Complex in Blessington, Co. Wicklow, travelling from as far away as Australia, Canada, Austria, Scotland and England. Others journeyed from Armagh, Westmeath, Kildare, Dublin and of course, from the family home down the road.

John and Mary Byrne married in 1920 and had 14 children, nine daughters and five sons. Val Byrne, the Chieftain of the O'Byrne clan, got the proceedings off the ground. This was followed by live music, a fine dinner, and the evening was rounded off nicely with a traditional game of cards.

THE MUD VISION
A reflection by Séamus Heaney

Séamus Heaney is one of Ireland's most celebrated poets.

*T*he Mud Vision is a poem embedded in memories of life in an older Ireland but it also gestures towards an Ireland that is still coming into being. It has its origins in certain specific incidents in my personal past and has its meaning in intimations of what seems to be happening in the national psyche, at present and for the future.

The poem is a dramatic monologue, spoken by a member of a community that has the trappings of modernity but not the spirit of it. Then all of a sudden the people are visited by an apparition in the sky, something that looks like a great wheel of spinning, airborne mud. This vision speaks to something deep in the people's make-up and attains a kind of religious aura for them, so as long as it is in evidence they experience a unique moment of self-belief, a kind of reawakening. Then the mud vision disappears and the people are back in a secular, workaday world.

Two experiences from my teenage years get worked into the story obliquely. Fundamental to the whole conception is the memory of the countryside in mid-Ulster in the 1950's – or the Catholic part of it at any rate – being brought alive by reports that the Virgin Mary had appeared to a woman in Ardboe in Co. Tyrone, on the shores of Lough Neagh. For a whole summer the by-roads around the place and the back garden of the woman's house were crowded with people excited by the prospect of the apparition happening again. Busloads came from as far away as Cork, young women entered convents, vendors of religious objects set up on the roadside. There was a surge of excitement, a big emotional wave and at the same time an opposite but not equal scepticism – an attitude approved by the clergy.

The second experience happened earlier. During a local dramatic society's production of a play that told the story of another apparition of the Virgin, this time to the three children at Fatima, a lighting effect occurred that was sudden, brilliant and unforgettable. Melodramatic too, representing the sun changing colour, as it was supposed to have changed at Fatima.

In the fiction of the poem, the person who speaks belongs to a community like those around Ardboe and Fatima – religious, rural, superstitious, bewildered by the strangeness of their vision but at the deepest level, at home with it. And yet the world that surrounds them is out of sympathy with all that: the people on the ground regard the secular commentary on what they have been through as 'jabber'. You could say they are people in whom the battle for the modern Irish soul is being fought. To quote something I once wrote about them in another context:

> *They have been sprung from the world of the awestruck gaze, where there was belief in miracle, the sun standing still and the sun changing colour... They have entered the world of media-speak and post-modernity. They've been displaced from a culture not unlike that of de Valera's Ireland – frugal, nativist and inward looking, but still tuned to a supernatural dimension; and they find themselves in a universe that is global, desacralised, consumerist...*

But what about the mud, you might ask. The vision is a semi-religious one, its shape like that of a rose window in a cathedral, and this was the shape that the artist Richard Long created on a wall of the Guinness Hop Store during the Rosc exhibition in 1984. Long dipped his hand in mud hundreds if not thousands of times to make a flower-face of mud-prints, and in the free ranging way of the imagination, my memory of it surfaced and coalesced with those other earlier occasions of wonder.

The poem ends with an intimation that there has been a loss of faith – not necessarily religious faith, more the people's faith in themselves. Disappointment is general. Heretofore they had belief and a unique revelation, now they are left with the trappings of modernity in a world they understand but are no longer at home with. Alienated from what has been brought upon them, they 'crowd in for the big explanations', rather like the Irish population in the wake of the Celtic Tiger, listening, bewildered, to experts. Economists. Regulators. Apologisers. Apologists.

THE MUD VISION

Statues with exposed hearts and barbed-wire crowns
Still stood in alcoves, hares flitted beneath
The dozing bellies of jets, our menu-writers
And punks with aerosol sprays held their own
With the best of them. Satellite link-ups
Wafted over us the blessings of popes, heliports
Maintained a charmed circle for idols on tour
And casualties on their stretchers. We sleepwalked
The line between panic and formulae, screentested
Our first native models and the last of the mummers,
Watching ourselves at a distance, advantaged
And airy as a man on a springboard
Who keeps limbering up because the man cannot dive.

And then in the foggy midlands it appeared,
Our mud vision, as if a rose window of mud
Had invented itself out of the glittery damp,
A gossamer wheel, concentric with its own hub
Of nebulous dirt, sullied yet lucent.
We had heard of the sun standing still and the sun
That changed colour, but we were vouchsafed
Original clay, transfigured and spinning.
And then the sunsets ran murky, the wiper
Could never entirely clean off the windscreen,
Reservoirs tasted of silt, a light fuzz
Accrued in the hair and the eyebrows, and some
Took to wearing a smudge on their foreheads
To be prepared for whatever. Vigils
Began to be kept around puddled gaps,
On altars bulrushes ousted the lilies
And a rota of invalids came and went
On beds they could lease placed in range of the shower.

A generation who had seen a sign!
Those nights when we stood in an umber dew and smelled
Mould in the verbena, or woke to a light
Furrow-breath on the pillow, when the talk
Was all about who had seen it and our fear
Was touched with a secret pride, only ourselves

63

Could be adequate then to our lives. When the rainbow
Curved flood-brown and ran like a water-rat's back
So that drivers on the hard shoulder switched off to watch,
We wished it away, and yet we presumed it a test
That would prove us beyond expectation.

We lived, of course, to learn the folly of that.
One day it was gone and the east gable
Where its trembling corolla had balanced
Was starkly a ruin again, with dandelions
Blowing high up on the ledges, and moss
That slumbered on through its increase. As cameras raked
The site from every angle, experts
Began their post factum jabber and all of us
Crowded in tight for the big explanations.
Just like that, we forgot that the vision was ours,
Our one chance to know the incomparable
And dive to a future. What might have been origin
We dissipated in news. The clarified place
Had retrieved neither us nor itself- except
You could say we survived. So say that, and watch us
Who had our chance to be mud-men, convinced and estranged,
Figure in our own eyes for the eyes of the world.

1987

(Above)
Dennis 'DK' Kane, a surfboard maker, left, from San Diego, California, with his first cousin, Andrew Jacob, oyster fisherman and painter, from Cape Cod.

(Below)
A view from The Great Blasket Islands.

Photographs:
Valerie O'Sullivan

THE BLASKET GATHERING
Gary Quinn

There is a treacherous stretch of the Atlantic that flows between the mainland and the Great Blasket Island. Lives have been lost and journeys ended here, but it's a place where magic happens too. Sixty years after the evacuation of the Blasket Islands, and in the week of the Blaskets and West Kerry gathering, two surfers, great-great-grandsons of Padraig Ó Cathain, the King of the Blaskets, chased waves and met for the first time.

Chasing them in turn was a US documentary crew — itself infused with the DNA of the island — led by director, Mark Covino, who, with an outsider's eye, helped shaped a very local tale for a documentary called *The Crest*.

The surfing cousins, Dennis 'DK' Kane (25), and Andrew Jacob (33), hadn't met before the trip. DK runs a surfboard company in California, where he shapes and builds boards. Andy is a commerical fisherman who loves to surf in New England, where painting surfboards is his passion. Their grandfathers had been brothers and best friends, but separated by their lives on the opposite sides of America, the cousins only met for the first time in Dingle. It was an awkward introduction, all caught on camera, but the boys hit it off, and the spark that the producers were searching for took hold.

Family members, John and Eliza Kane, produced *The Crest*. They wanted to forge a story from the island — but they wanted to make something bigger than just their own family tale. They saw a hunger for identity in the US right now, particularly among the second and third generations. "We are American through and through, but there's this layered generation that fosters a feeling of, 'I want to go to that place'. People want to find out where their family have come from," Eliza explained. "And it's this we're trying to capture. This search for connection."

Andy and DK made connections all over the Dingle peninsula during their visit. The night before they chased waves together on the Blaskets they were locked into a pub in Dingle town, grabbing three hours sleep before our meeting in the Great Blasket Centre at Dún Chaoin. The island was behind us as we talked. A hare ran across the grass. Birds flew in the air and the sun shone hard upon the sculpture of the fisherman outside. DK said this trip had been the single most exciting experience of his life. He was bursting with pride, and his tales of his few days with his new brother-in-arms tripped over themselves.

Mark Covino, film director, left, Joe Spurr, camera operator, pictured making the film documentary.

Photograph: Valerie O'Sullivan

Getting to the Great Blasket was the peak, however. They had both tried and failed in the past, and now they stood together on the ferry, side by side in the rain. They took turns when they got there: the first to land, the first to enter the King's house, the first to catch a wave, the first to cliff-dive into the warm Atlantic. "It was like a Blasket baptism," Andy said laughing. "The rain stopped when we arrived. A group of donkeys came down to meet us. Seals splashed in the surf. It was like coming home."

They mounted their surfboards and paddled along cliff faces, into caves and under arches, knowing that they were seeing parts of the island very few people got to see. They stood in the King's house and looked through his window, staring at the same view he would have seen. The house is tiny, they say. Someone left a mattress there, some graffiti. They felt they should go back and fix it up.

They saw parallels everywhere. The racks holding the *naomhógs* (traditional Irish boats) that resemble DK's surfboard racks in his workshop back home; the remains of the fishing industry that mimic Andy's life in New England. They wanted to be at home, and they were. And proud of it.

They painted two surfboards at the King's house, not knowing they were being watched by another former islandman – Mike Carney, the oldest living islander, who was visiting the island, as he put it, for the last time. On the ferry home they talked to him and to the descendants of Robin Flowers, the British writer and folklorist who came to the island in 1910 to document the literature and life there – so many descendants gathered together at one time. A small flicker of history passed between them, and then they separated again in Dingle. But the two men from America felt bigger because of it, and somehow humbled by their experience, they said. Their smiles have not gone away.

Reunion is very seductive, particularly when one is trying to forge something un-known. It is, in essence, what *The Gathering* is for – to bring home those people who have become stories themselves: the emigrants and their descendants. It is exciting and poignant all at the same time, full of sadness and loss but well worth gathering for.

Gary Quinn is a travel writer with The Irish Times.

A view of the Blasket Islands from Slea Head, Dingle Peninsula, Co. Kerry.

Photograph: Valerie O'Sullivan

RETURNING HOME
Anne Lucey

It was an emotional day when, at the age of 93, the oldest living Blasket islander, Michael Carney (in Irish, Micheál O'Cearna), made a return journey from America to the island where he was reared.

With tears in his eyes, Michael (known as Mike to his friends) looked around the deserted Great Blasket Island, 76 years after he first left at the age of 17. He took in the ruins of his old village and remembered how he spent endless hours playing football with his friends.

Michael was acccompanied on this very special journey by his sons, daughters, son-in-law and grandchildren.

Born in 1920, Michael spent much of his life in the US, but he always maintained strong links with west Kerry. His trip to his native island coincided with the launch of his memoirs at the Blasket Island interpretive centre at Dún Chaoin and a special gathering of surviving native islanders.

During his visit Michael recalled his childhood and his decision to leave the island and its isolation in 1937 to seek a better future in Dublin and eventually in America. He spoke no English when he left, and continues to speak Irish.

The Great Blasket, now an uninhabited, treeless island overlooking the Atlantic, was abandoned 60 years ago after life became impossible for the handful of islanders left there.

Anne Lucey is a journalist and writer based in the South West.

(Opposite)
Michael Carney (93) on his
return to the Blasket Islands.

Photograph: Valerie O'Sullivan

Photographs: Joe Keogh /
Keogh Photography

ON BEING BRIDGET MARY
A reflection by Bridget Megarry

Bridget Megarry is a former teacher who lives in Dublin.

My names were a problem to me growing up. My father was reared in England but returned to his father's family for holidays in Ireland. He was determined that his youngest daughter would have Irish names, and was suitably gratified that I had curly reddish-blond hair, freckles and a love of potatoes.

As a result I felt different from the start, but I adored my father, and anything that earned his attention was fine by me. In Ireland on holidays being Bridget was no problem. But when my looks and names provoked ridicule in the playground of my English state primary school, I realised that being called 'Irish' wasn't always a compliment.

The latter part of my teens and young adult life were spent in East Africa. It was here that I grew up, began my teaching career and fell in love with a man who had been born in Chile to Anglo-Irish parents. Like me, he had an English accent but an Irish name. He had been reared and schooled in Ireland so felt it was 'home'.

We were fortunate in the early 1980's, when jobs were scarce, that Kevin was offered a job in Dublin. So back we came to an Irish winter, buying a new house in Dublin where we still live. I thought I would die of the cold and the damp and the loneliness. I missed the sun and my African way of life so much it hurt.

However I soon settled down. Being Bridget meant being part of an Irish community – 'Bridie' to my husband, 'Ma' to my children, 'Mrs Megarry' to my students and

73

Bridget to work colleagues and friends. I loved it. For the first time in my life, I felt I belonged somewhere. However, it is perhaps only now that I fully appreciate what that community fellowship and sense of belonging means.

In September 2012 I was diagnosed with a rare form of bone marrow cancer. I've recently had a bone marrow transplant but the odds of my surviving the process disease-free are against me. Only about 20% of people with my condition who undergo a transplant survive to live healthy lives. I am currently undergoing treatment which is preventing the disease from progressing, but it may reverse at any time and my prognosis with or without the treatment is not good. I am 58 years old. It is unlikely I will live to celebrate my 60th birthday.

How does one live with such a diagnosis? It wasn't part of the plan. We are on the cusp of retirement. Our youngest child has just spread her wings and has found herself a good job in London and the older married ones are starting to produce grandchildren, whom I adore.

I love babies and small children and planned to be a 'hands on' grandma. I was looking forward to fun breaks with my now adult daughter and, in due course, helping her to choose her wedding dress. An adventurous road trip to India was being planned with my younger son. Seven years ago we bought a house in our favourite corner of France where we had hoped to spend much of our retirement, welcoming our children and theirs to sunny holidays and the French way of life. We enjoy living in Dublin but love the contrast and quiet of rural France.

Thus, we had reached a time where a new chapter of our lives was about to begin and we were excited about it.

There are no words to describe the grief and sense of loss I am experiencing, knowing that there's little chance of being part of that future.

Suddenly, it all looks very different. Being Bridget Mary means being someone who is terminally ill. I spend a lot of time in hospital where my identity is defined not only by my name but by a hospital number. My work life has come to an abrupt end. I have to exclude myself from many of my leisure activities (book club, French class, theatre and cinema, etc) due to the risk of infection. But my family, friends and community remain constant.

I am surrounded by love. Meals, cakes, biscuits, cards and emails arrive daily. Friends from England and France come to stay. Our children text or ring daily and come home as often as they can. The hospital system is incredible. Yes, the waiting periods for treatment are long. The Accident & Emergency Department is a nightmare (I'm terrified I'm going to die on a trolley), but the level of care, kindness and expertise is second to none. I have nothing but praise for the wonderful nurses, doctors and consultants who are looking after me.

I am learning to restrict my 'things to look forward to', just in case. At the end of April 2013, all our children, wives and grandchildren came home. We had a week together, our own special gathering for the year that's in it. The economic climate has allowed only one son and his family to work in Ireland, the rest are scattered around the world, so to have them all together under our roof was wonderful.

I have a lot of time to reflect. I think about my names and how they have defined who I am. Who were these women I was named after and how did they cope with adversity? How might they have reacted to the situation I find myself in?

The more I find out about St Brigid the prouder I become that I bear her name. It seems she was a strong woman, a multi-tasker, tough when she needed to be but compassionate and kind, with a deep faith. My favourite of her blessings suggests that, like me, she found value in a good party and in preparing feasts for her family and friends with good food and plenty to drink.

I should like a great lake of finest ale
for the King of Kings.
I should like a tableful of choicest food
for the family of heaven.
Let the ale be made from the fruits of faith and the food of forgiving love.
I should welcome the poor to my feast,
for they are God's children.
I should welcome the sick to my feast,
for they are God's joy.
Let the poor sit with Jesus at the highest place,
and the sick dance with the angels.

(An Ancient Song to St Brigid from Celtic Fire by Robert Van de Weyer (1991)).

I have good and bad days and experience dark chasms of despair when my head is full of fear and questions. Will I be in the lucky 20% and get to live more life? How will I cope with the pain and suffering of invasive hospital treatment and, when it comes, the process of dying? How will the family manage without me? I so want to leave them the legacy of remembering me in these times as having courage and dignity. How can I do this without my grief overwhelming me?

My faith helps. Having been raised in the Anglo-Catholic tradition I sometimes find the Church of Ireland practices of my husband's tradition challenge my own creed, where Mary has greater significance. Mary, the mother of Jesus, Mary of the Magnificat, Mary after whom I was named. Perhaps Paul McCartney says it best:

When I find myself in times of trouble, Mother Mary comes to me,
Singing words of wisdom, let it be,
And in my hour of darkness she is standing right in front of me,
Whispering words of wisdom, let it be,
Let it be, let it be, let it be, let it be.
Whispering words of wisdom, let it be.

The Megarry Family.

Photograph: Chris Bellew /
Fennell Photography

THE HIDE-AND-SEEK CHILDREN
Lynn Jackson

In 1948, a group of 100 Jewish Slovak children who had survived the Holocaust were granted temporary visas to spend one year of respite and recovery in Ireland. They stayed in Clonyn Castle, in Co. Westmeath.

All the arrangements for their stay, including the procurement of the castle and transporting of the children from Europe, was organised by Rabbi Dr Solomon Schonfeld, a man who worked tirelessly to save Jewish lives and to help retain Jewish heritage before, during and after the war. His task in bringing the Holocaust children to Ireland was not easy, and he had to overcome many obstacles, including government reluctance to allow the children to come in the first place. He even managed to persuade his friend, Jacob Levy from Manchester, to purchase Clonyn Castle for use as a temporary children's home – a project that ultimately contributed to his bankruptcy.

Barbara Barnett chronicles the story of some of the children who came to Ireland, the year they spent in the castle and what happened to them afterwards in her book *The Hide-And-Seek Children*.

David Rosenfield, who was nine years old when he was in Ireland, recalls in the book, "It was like paradise", while Murray Lynn, who, at 18, was one of the oldest, remarks, "Clonyn Castle was where we were cared for and cared about."

The new arrivals played with the local children in Delvin, where they learned English and some childhood games, including hide-and-seek. Most of the children enjoyed this game, but for some it was too unnerving, and reminded them of the fear they had experienced in hiding from, being hunted by, and ultimately being captured by the Nazis.

Many of the children who came to Ireland were the only members of their entire families to survive Nazi concentration or death camps. Others had been 'hidden' during the war, entrusted to non-Jews by their parents in the hope of saving their lives. They were sheltered by partisans, priests, nuns, peasants and professionals. They lived under false identities, with or without forged papers, in unfamiliar surroundings and at constant risk of detection. Any discovery of their true identities could bring certain death – not just for them, but also for their courageous protectors.

In her book, Barnett reflects that as their year came to a close, the older children especially were anxious to complete their education or to learn a trade or profession – they were ready to move on. They were fully at ease with the English language, and perhaps their young age when their lives fell apart was to their advantage. They had the natural urge of healthy young people to look ahead and think positively – something far more difficult for survivors of a mature age.

None of the 'Hide-and-Seek Children' went back to Slovakia, where the new Communist government had forbidden all religious practice. They scattered to many parts of the world including the newly created state of Israel, North America, Australia or England.

And so, it was with great poignancy that six of the children came back to Ireland after 65 years, and met each other again in a very special gathering event, organised by Holocaust Education Trust Ireland. There was a collective gasp of, "The castle!", as it loomed into view, and excitement as the group pointed to various windows and recalled soccer games in the front fields.

So many memories and stories spilled out.

It seemed that the entire village of Delvin had gathered in St Patrick's Hall to welcome Murray Lynn, David Rosenfield, Vera Steiner, Mareka Gutmann, Jerry Weiser and Eva Wiesenfeld, to rapturous applause and cheering. The daughter of the milkman, Andy Leonard, bought a copy of Barbara's book for her father; the cook's daughter had great stories from her mum about the children. The villagers remembered the children lining up for their first pair of plimsolls from Clark's shoeshop – something of their very own.

The day went on, with too many stories and too many memories to squeeze into a mere afternoon. Delvin did Ireland proud with the wonderful warm reception, Irish music and dancing and personal anecdotes.

Eva's daughter, Judith Weiss, who accompanied her mother said: "Having experienced this outpouring of friendship from total strangers, I am convinced that if enough people like you were in Europe 70 years ago, the horrors of the Holocaust may not have been able to happen." Mareka Gutmann had been in two minds about whether she should come back to Ireland, but said she was so glad she made the journey and remarked that it was "truly amazing and very emotional." Murray said that the 'Hide-and-Seek' event was a heart-warming and deeply emotional experience. "I will always cherish and long remember the milk of human kindness."

The three-day gathering event culminated in a public meeting at the RDS. More reminiscences were evoked and memories revealed. Everyone involved in the event had come face to face with children who had survived the Holocaust; they heard stories to recount to their children, grandchildren and to future generations.

It is Ireland's loss that the 'Hide-and-Seek Children' were not allowed to remain in Ireland. They would undoubtedly have made a very positive contribution to all walks of Irish life, as well as to the Irish Jewish community.

Lynn Jackson is the Director of Education at Holocaust Education Trust Ireland.

(Below)
Clonyn Castle Football team and supporters, courtesy of Barbara Barnett. David Rosenfeld, one of the Hide-and-Seek Children who returned for the event is pictured, in the middle of the back row, wearing a black hat and jumper.

(Left)
David Rosenfield,
Mareka Gutmann,
Eva Wiesenfeld,
Barbara Barnett,
Murray Lynn,
Vera Steiner,
Jerry Weiser.

Photograph:
Sharon Jackson

Red Coats (British Army) open fire on the rebels during the re-enactment of the Battle of Vinegar Hill which took place during the Irish Rebellion of 1798 Enniscorthy Co. Wexford.

Photograph: Brenda Fitzsimons / The Irish Times

GATHERING HOME THOUGHTS FROM ABROAD

A reflection by Tim O'Connor

Tim O'Connor currently chairs the Project Advisory Board for The Gathering 2013.

Growing up in rural west Limerick in the 1950's and 1960's, emigration was all around. Not that we called it by that name. People leaving was just a painful fact of life. John B. Keane found words for it, though. Powerful words. One Lenten Sunday night in Cronin's Hall in Killeedy, I saw *Many Young Men of Twenty* and was mesmerised by the punch it packed. I have never forgotten its rawness.

Much later, I got my own qualified taste of emigration, when I joined the Department of Foreign Affairs and signed up for a life on the move. My first posting was at the Irish Embassy in Bonn, the then capital of West Germany, in the early 1980's. I say "qualified" because it was a very protected kind of emigration, working for Ireland, surrounded by Irish colleagues and with lots of support in various ways. But it was still four years in a foreign country, speaking a foreign language and far from the familiarities of home. And for the early stages certainly, I found it tough going. I got an inkling of what it must have been like for millions of our people over the years who had no choice, and none of the support that I had, in packing up their lives, uprooting themselves from home, community and past, and beginning again in a new world, often thousands of miles away, with no prospect of return. A respect for the emigrant was born.

But it was as Consul General of Ireland in New York from 2005-2007 that I experienced the full force of another dimension of our emigration experience – the extraordinary impact of the Irish in their adopted lands. In New York, the Irish influence is literally everywhere. Our people helped build that city. Over the years, they have run

81

most of the things that make it tick – the police, the fire department, the labour unions, the building industry, and of course the politics. In latter generations, the Irish have spread their way across the professions – the law, medicine, media, business, the judiciary, academia, Wall Street. And our influence is biggest of all on another great New York street – Broadway. The cumulative result is that the mark of Ireland in that city is all-pervasive, symbolised by the way it comes to a standstill – or marches to our drum-beat – on St Patrick's Day. For me, that was where respect turned to a kind of awe.

That is why I see *The Gathering* as such a powerful project. I believe that our relationship with our diaspora – our global community, now estimated to run to 70 million people – is a critical dimension of the Ireland story, to be cherished and nurtured. To mutual benefit. That is a key design requirement. When *The Gathering* was being planned, the actor Gabriel Byrne warned against the danger of an approach that could be construed as "user". He was right. Our relationship with the diaspora must be one of mutuality of respect and interests. *The Gathering* is all about mutuality.

I had the honour to work as Secretary General to the President during part of the tenure of President McAleese and saw at first hand the impact she had in visiting numerous Irish communities overseas. I was particularly struck by a powerful image she used, suggesting that the Irish emigrant in effect had two hearts – one for the adopted land and one for Ireland, the latter never ceasing to pulse strongly. President Higgins has maintained this deep focus on the global Irish during his term to date.

What makes *The Gathering* different as an initiative is that it is a 'People's Project'. Without the involvement and participation of the people of Ireland, *The Gathering* would not be the success it is. *The Gathering* takes the diaspora issue back down to where the emigrant journeys began – the farmsteads, homes, parishes, villages and towns of Ireland. Instead of the Government doing the reaching out to the general diaspora, it is the individual communities and families reaching out to their kith and fellow parishioners abroad, saying 'we invite you, we welcome you home, tell us your story, we celebrate you and our common kinship'.

It turns out that this is something very powerful. I was privileged to be part of a ceremony at Siamsa Tíre in Tralee where Kerry County Council honoured Dr Kevin Cahill, a distinguished New York physician, academic and writer, whose grandfather had left Kerry, bound for Ellis Island, in 1895. It was a wonderful gathering where the Home Place reached out to, listened to the story of, and celebrated the emigrant journey of one of their own. Dr Cahill has received about 35 honorary doctorates in his illustrious career. One of his sons said to me after the Siamsa event that that ceremony was probably the most meaningful award of all for his father. Some statement!

All this brings me to a key learning as far as I'm concerned, from working on *The Gathering*. It is this: if the relationship between Ireland and its 70 million global community is going to go to a deeper level, a large responsibility rests in the first place with us who live in Ireland. Why? Because we are the keepers of the 'Home Place'.

My analogy is a simple one – the country farm with the large family, say ten children. All the offspring grow up on the land together, working the farm, a closely bonded unit. But only one sibling inherits, with the other nine scattering, and from that moment on the sense of connection to the home and farm of that family hugely depends on the sibling who has inherited. So it is with Ireland and our 70 million diaspora. We who live in Ireland are the keepers of the Home Place. Much depends on us as the keepers, the custodians. Plus, we keep one other important dimension – we are the keepers of the graves of the previous generations of those who left.

The Gathering is a powerful project of its time. As Ireland approaches its 100th birthday as an independent country, this is surely the moment and the opportunity to be engaged in closing the circle around those who stayed and those who left. If we do, we will all be the richer.

In addition to the powerful psychological impact of closing that circle with a community of people who are an integral part of us, we at home will be creating for ourselves a great global community and network of support, based on mutual respect and trust, that will be a huge asset as we continue, in a brutally globalised world, the painful journey of national recovery.

The Gathering demonstrates the lift that can hold for our tourism and hospitality sectors starting with that extraordinary home coming of 35,000 Irish Americans in September 2012 for the Notre Dame v Navy game. And those living outside, and the descendants of those who had to leave, will know in a new way that their heritage – and the graves of their ancestors – are in safe and respectful keeping, in a place which in a real way will always be home for them and where there they will always find a special welcome. That is the prize and value of *The Gathering*. And a fitting mark of respect to every single one of John B.'s *Many Young Men (and Women) of Twenty* who had to say goodbye.

BALLINCOOLA MURPHY GATHERING
Wexford

(Top)
'A Mustering of Murphys'.

Photograph: Shay Doyle

(Below)
Grandfather and
Grandmother Murphy.

The sudden apparition of a group of people in Curracloe graveyard in Co. Wexford early one morning raised an eyebrow or two among the locals. However, fears of any sinister goings-on were quickly dispelled when it emerged that it was members of the 80-strong Murphy clan paying a visit.

Invitations to this gathering were limited to direct descendants of grandparents, Raymond and Ciss Murphy. A 30-foot family tree, dating as far back as 'Reddy the Bonesetter' in 1809, was put together. A branch of relatives completely lost to memory was unearthed, while the discovery of Father Patrick Murphy and his work in the first Carmelite monastery in Australia also brought much pride to those in attendance.

Father Patrick's missal, altar stone dating from Penal Times, his chalice and some of his letters were among a wealth of family memorabilia on display over the weekend.

KALEIDOSCOPE

A reflection by Rosita Boland

Rosita Boland is a journalist with The Irish Times.

My beat as a features writer for *The Irish Times* over many years has taken me all over Ireland. I've interviewed people on streets, in fields, in offices, kitchens and living rooms, in an enclosed convent where I couldn't clearly see my interviewees behind the screen that shadowed them, in schools, prisons, pubs and funeral parlours, backstage at theatres, on a Sligo beach where everyone was naked prior to a charity swim, in a derelict windowless castle in Louth where I slept on straw and ate only foraged food for a grim five days with seven others while reporting on a 'living history' experiment, in a rowing boat on a lake in Leitrim during torrential rain while an actor performed a monologue, when carrying a hawk on my wrist while with falconers in Mayo, and once when I was half-asleep, interviewing shoppers at 4am in the first all-night supermarket to open in Dublin.

I've interviewed probably thousands of people, and of course some remain more sharply in my memory than others. But they all still have something in common. By allowing themselves to be interviewed, collectively these people have given me fascinating and often moving glimpses into other lives that compose a kaleidoscope of Ireland, past and present.

One of the first ideas I had for a feature was to report on the many items held in storage at the National Museum. Why, I wondered, were some objects deemed not good enough to go on display, but yet to be kept?

I can still recall the grey steel cabinet that was silently opened for me in one of the many storage rooms at Collins Barracks. Within were several large silver trophies, cups and bowls, some quite badly dented. They were not held in national storage, I was told, because of either their craftsmanship or rarity.

They all had inscriptions. As I read, something like horror descended. Here were inscriptions for hunting trophies won in the years 1845, 1846, 1847. While many starved during the Famine, there were of course others who did not, a fact I had never thought about much until that moment. The wealthy continued to hunt, and win silver trophies, and go on with their lives. The cabinet was a haunting and powerful example of unseen objects bearing witness to our social history.

In 2004, I went to Loch Na Fooey in Connemara for part of a series I was writing on crafts. Joe Hogan is a master craftsman; a basket-maker who has been making exquisite and functional baskets since 1978 with willows he grows on his own land. He sat on the floor of his workshop, weaving as he talked about how he had learned his craft. Sitting, he said, was the best position to be in for basket weaving (although I suspect not the best position for a human back).

Watching him, I was so mesmerised I almost forgot I was meant to be interviewing him. The way his hands worked the willows reminded me of birds instinctively building nests.

Two years ago, when I moved house, I contacted Joe Hogan and commissioned him to make a turf basket for my new home. It arrived splendidly one day to the office, like a dandelion clock drifting to land. Amazingly, there was no wrapping and no packaging – just a hand-written label with a stamp on it tied to one of the handles, and all who saw my basket that day marvelled. It was as if it had flown through the air to Dublin, blown straight from Joe Hogan's hands. Since then, there has been a living piece of Connemara by my fire.

In 2010, I was on my way to Cahersiveen in Co. Kerry to interview the meteorologists who monitor the Valentia Island station. I did interview them, but not before I stumbled, unplanned, upon another story en route. Or rather, not stumbled but drove my way into another story.

While I was diverting to follow a sign for Bowen's Court in Farahy, Co. Cork – the home of novelist, Elizabeth Bowen – the track ran out, and my car got wedged in a ploughed field. I could not get it out, and to my amazement, nobody I flagged down on the rural road offered to help. Where, I wrote later, was 'Ireland of the Welcomes' on that afternoon? One car that reluctantly stopped told me to call the guards, as if the driver considered that it was from representatives of state bodies, and not honest-to-God passers-by, that I should be looking for help.

I eventually knocked on the door of Arthur and Brenda Hennessy in near despair. Until that afternoon, I had taken it for granted that I lived in a country where kindliness to strangers in need and an informal code of decency was the norm. The Hennessys restored that faith to me. They helped me pull the car out of the field, while getting spectacularly covered in mud themselves. Arthur insisted on washing my car and muddy boots, while Brenda insisted I come in for tea.

The piece I later wrote about the incident generated a huge response from readers: "Thankfully," one reader's heartfelt comment went, "we still have Arthurs and Brendas in Ireland."

Joe Hogan

Photograph: Courtesy of Joe Hogan / CCoI

TRIP OF A LIFETIME
Pierce Kent

38 years later, Pierce Kent and his wife Kate return to the place where they first met outside the Bank of Ireland in College Green, Dublin.

I first became aware of *The Gathering* in early autumn 2012, as I was sitting at home in Michigan, watching my favourite college American football team, Notre Dame, play Navy at the Aviva Stadium in my native Dublin on TV. Commercials shown during breaks in the action referred to *The Gathering*. A day or two later, when surfing the web, I came across an invitation on *The Gathering* website to enter a competition with the prize of a trip for four to Ireland.

Entrants had to say in 300 words why they should be invited to Ireland for *The Gathering*. I wrote about how I met my lovely American wife in the winter of 1975 outside the Bank of Ireland on College Green in Dublin. I had missed a law exam, having turned up to an empty exam hall in the afternoon, not realising that the test had taken place that morning. I was unhappy as I had really crammed for the test. I bumped into a family friend and his new wife, and we went drinking, helping me forget my woes.

I set eyes upon the green-eyed American woman whom I was to fall in love with and marry later that year. Kate was very friendly and we got chatting. I invited her for a cup of coffee, and we went to a pub then known as Brannigans, on Parnell Street, where the cup of coffee was soon forgotten and stronger beverages were enjoyed. Kate was a wonderful drinking companion and delightful company.

In my entry for the competition, I mentioned this first encounter and the fact that, as a keen genealogist and amateur historian, I had traced her father's family roots back to Co. Roscommon. Kate's maiden name is Conley, and Conley is one of the many anglicised variations of the Irish name, Ó Conghaile.

I was ecstatic when I won the competition. As well as Kate, I asked Pat, widow of my late friend, James, to come to Ireland with us along with her sister Eileen. Pat is a native Michigander with Irish roots who first met her husband in Durty Nelly's pub in Bunratty, Co. Clare, when she was in Ireland as a tourist in 1977. Another sister of Pat's, Edna, and her husband, Jim, travelled on the same flight as us from Chicago to Dublin, making up great company for our special homecoming journey.

Our *Gathering* prize was for a week, and we stayed in wonderful hotel accommodation in Dublin, Athlone, Castlebar and Enniscrone. We packed in a lot of sightseeing, highlights including visits to Kilmainham Gaol, Joyce's Tower in Sandycove, Clonmacnoise, Athlone Castle, the Deserted Famine Village on Achill and the Céide Fields on the coast of north Mayo, soon to be a UNESCO world heritage site. We enjoyed delightful pubs and eating places.

For our good friend Pat, there was a sentimental trip to Durty Nelly's in Bunratty. The day we visited there were three dolphins cavorting in the tidal river outside the pub, which had drawn hundreds of onlookers to the village.

We had a very special visit to my former home in Balbriggan, Co. Dublin. When Kate and I first met I took Kate to visit there several times. The first time stands out. My father served her a boiled egg for breakfast and placed it in an egg cup, as is usual in Ireland. But this is not the custom in Kate's home state of Michigan. She removed the egg from the cup and proceeded to crack it open with a spoon, which bemused my father and me.

On our gathering trip we spent a night at the Bracken Hotel in Balbriggan and visited the nearby Donore Hills graveyard, looking for the gravestone of Kate's six-times great-grandfather, Luke Conoly. After an evening meal in the hotel we wandered up to my father's old house. Kate took a photograph, and because it was dark, the camera flash drew the attention of Johnny Fortune's son-in-law. I told him that I had lived in the house some years ago. He invited us both in to meet Johnny, his wife and daughter. We had a lovely visit and were served cups of tea and apple tart. The Fortunes were a great advertisement for Irish hospitality.

Kate has stood by me through the rough and the smooth for 38 years. We have two lovely daughters Siobhán and Mary Brigid, or Bridie as we call her. I had serious health setbacks and two major surgeries in recent years, but thankfully I was fully recovered and ready for the trip back to my native land.

The Gathering prize meant the world to Kate and myself, and also to our friends, Pat and Eileen.

Go raibh míle maith agaibh.

Pierce Kent was the winner of a Gathering Ireland 2013 trip to Ireland.

DUAL CITIZENSHIP
A reflection by Michael Kearney

Irish-born Michael Kearney lives in Santa Barbara, California and works as a palliative care and hospice physician.

The word 'indigenous' means being 'native to' or 'born within' a particular place. The opposite of indigenous is 'foreign' or 'alien'. I am an Irishman who has been living in the US for over 10 years. I have come into a deep relationship with this land, especially through contact with Native American teachers, which has, somewhat unexpectedly, led me into a deeper sense of what it means to be Irish and a new kind of relationship with Ireland.

There is no nostalgia and I do not pine to return to live in Ireland. And yet, I feel more Irish now than I ever did when I lived there. I have discovered what it means to be Irish by becoming familiar with the place that Native Americans call '*Turtle Island*', this American land.

In February 2013 I took US citizenship, and sat with 2,500 other people in the Los Angeles Convention Center at the swearing-in ceremony, with an 80-year-old Colombian woman to my left and an 80-year old Iranian man to my right. Shortly afterwards I travelled to Ireland with my new American passport in one pocket and my Irish passport in the other.

As I have become more and more connected to this place, to this American land, my own sense of Irishness has awakened. How could this be? I believe that it is because my introduction to this place was through those who are indigenous here, those who intimately know and are known by this land. Their Native American ceremonies have

enabled me to come into deep connection with 'all my relations'. But why did this process not result in my becoming more American in some generic, melted-down sort of way? Why, instead, am I feeling more Irish?

Insights from schools of thought as diverse as Buddhist philosophy and General Systems Theory reveal that the flow of energy and information between different parts of an open system does not lead to sameness or uniformity of those parts, but to their becoming ever more differentiated and particular.

Think of two lovers who, in their togetherness, become more distinctively themselves. Think of parts of the brain, which, through the constant exchange of energy and information, evolve into more and more sophisticated differentiation. Or, think of an owl and a mouse in a forest. Their interactions over time do not make the owl more mouse-like and the mouse more owl-like. On the contrary; owl becomes more owl, evolving soft inner rims to her feathers for silent flight and swooping on mouse, and mouse becomes more mouse, literally, having up to 12 young in each of her six litters a year to outnumber owl's manoeuvres.

Chumash Indian rock design, Red Tail Hawk feather, and "White Sage".

Photograph: Michael Kearney

With the help of those who are indigenous to this place I have come into a deep relationship with this American land. And, as I have come home to the dynamic web of information and energy that is the American experience, I have changed from being a 'permanent resident alien' to being a citizen, and more the Irishman I am than I ever was. Dual citizenship seems the way to go.

DRAMA IN WICKLOW GAOL
Terry Dunne

My wife's brother, Gay Collins, originally from Cambo, Croghan, Doyle in Co. Roscommon, lives in Perth with his wife Martine and four children. When he decided to come home for *The Gathering*, he wanted something special organised so that his family would never forget the trip. We happily obliged!

Gay was told that the 'special' event would involve a visit to the National Heritage Park in Wexford, with a marching band, a meal and traditional music.

We never did make it to Wexford. Instead, as soon as Gay and his family arrived at our house in Wicklow Town, we had them 'arrested' and brought to Wicklow Historic Gaol, where they were tried, convicted and deported back to Perth. We even had real Gardaí (some off-duty friends) carry out the arrests.

Poor Gay completely fell for it! For the trial, his brother acted as the prosecutor; I played the role of court clerk, while a friend was the judge. The family, which included other members who had travelled from Australia and the UK for the occasion, were the jury.

It was a huge success, and all thanks to Wicklow Gaol, which provided the venue and the gaoler.

(Above and overleaf)
The "arrest, charge and trial" of
Gay Collins.

Photographs:
Brendan Cullen

THE FOUR PILLARS
A reflection by Pearse and Deirdre Lyons

Pearse and Deirdre Lyons are the Irish couple behind one of the world's leading animal health and nutrition companies, Alltech.

PEARSE:

Like any Irish person who works abroad, I am intensely proud of my home, of its unique identity and its rich history. But most of all, I am proud of Irish people, of what we have achieved and can yet achieve.

The tentacles of the Irish spread all over the globe, and *The Gathering* is a unique opportunity to bring people back home to connect, reach out and share experiences. And nowhere more than in the world of business celebrating our Irish tradition of international commerce and trade.

Sometimes it feels like we arrived in America only days ago, yet we have been here for over 30 years. It has been a great journey, coming from a different background, with a different way of looking at things, a different education and different ambitions.

It is often said jokingly that there are two types of people in the world: those who are Irish, and those who wish to be Irish. The Irish are a formidable lot. 'The Fighting Irish' of Notre Dame are perhaps the best known college football team in America. They are always a force to be reckoned with and the ones to beat in any field. Every game is tough when a team is playing the Irish.

America has embraced the Irish – their way of life, and their history of fighting for their rights. That is why it is great to be Irish in America.

St Patrick's Day in particular is incredible. It is a day which many Irish at home think is restricted to Chicago, New York, and San Francisco – the big cities. But it is celebrated everywhere – even in Lexington, Kentucky, our home. Savannah, Georgia, celebrates the Irish rebel Kevin Barry, and the whole city closes down each 17th March.

We have Irish dancing everywhere, and as our company representatives travel the country, and indeed the world, often Irish dancers are the showstopper. Our son, Mark, who lives in China, called me excitedly on St. Patrick's Day and said: "Dad, we've got Irish dancers." Big deal, I thought – but the big deal was that the Irish dancers were Chinese!

So what is it like to be Irish here? It is having a door open. You have a name that is easy to pronounce. I have often said that the Irish have never beaten anybody in battle because we are the eternal underdogs – and everyone loves an underdog. Everybody particularly likes an underdog who is successful, who will go out of his or her way to help you – providing you never lose the common touch. The common touch is uniquely Irish. "Remember where you come from," my mum used to say, "and don't fly too high."

DEIRDRE:

We live in Kentucky, a glorious place with rolling hills, verdant pastures and beautiful horses. But even though Kentucky is our adopted home, our hearts will always be in Ireland.

Everyone in the US claims to have some Irish connection, and love being around the Irish for the *craic* and good times. Kentucky is home to many Irish working in the equine industry – vets, trainers, riders, grooms and indeed, horse farm owners – so we stay connected to home through them.

Lexington in Kentucky has had a St Patrick's Day parade since 1980, started by a generous Irish man, Bill Enright. This has become the highlight of mid-spring, with weather that can range from sunny and 60°F, to cold with light snow. No matter what the weather, families love this event for its fun and inclusiveness. It is a great gathering of the Irish and all those wanting to be Irish for the day.

We Irish love to sing – some of us not so well, mind you, but nevertheless, we join in! Pearse and I have made music part of our lives in Kentucky. In 2006 we set up a music scholarship at the University of Kentucky's Opera Theatre Department with director, Everett McCorvey. It takes place on the first Sunday of every March, and attracts students from as far away as Brazil and Ecuador. From seed money of $25,000 in 2006, the competition now gives away scholarships topping over $500,000.

It is so satisfying for us to see young people from all over the world live their dream. The Irish tenor, Ronan Tynan, is now a visiting professor at the University of Kentucky School of Music, and many Lexingtonians look forward to his visits.

The Irish are a generous people, and no matter what hard times they have been through, they are always there to help their own — and others — in time of need. One example of how the Irish reach out was after the hurricane in Haiti, when they got involved in lots of the relief effort. We invited our first graduate scholarship winner, Eric Brown, to visit Haiti and help us form the Haiti Children's Choir. Eric worked with 30 children for over three months, and we brought them to Kentucky for the opening ceremonies of the Alltech World Equestrian Games in 2010. The experience these children had was amazing. They even had the magic of appearing on-stage with Paddy Moloney and the Chieftains and Ronan Tynan.

The four pillars of our life and business are education, innovation, application and philanthropy. We believe these are what make us essentially Irish — the desire to share and give a step up the ladder in the hope that the idea will spread and keep spreading.

When I fondly think of Ireland, I think of Ashford Castle; Joyce country; Connemara; the Phoenix Park; the National Botanic Gardens; afternoon tea in the Shelbourne, followed by a walk in St Stephen's Green; the Feather Beds and the Sally Gap in Wicklow. And of course … family and friends! There is nothing like being Irish and nothing like coming home.

The Inagh Valley, Connemara.

Photograph: Philip Campbell

DESCENDANTS OF THE GREAT HOUSES
Anne Lucey

Gatherings in Kerry have meant a sometimes painful past. But the first gathering in over 100 years of the descendants of the great houses of the south-west, held in majestic Muckross House in Killarney, was a joyful occasion.

The titles on the guest list for this special event reflected the very Irish character of what is meant by the 'nobility' here. Most of the gentry in the south-west had come to Ireland from England and Scotland under land grants from the English Crown in the 16th and 17th centuries. Some of the native Irish, however particularly the Catholic gentry – were allowed to keep their lands because of strategic alliances. Thus, representatives of the 'McGillycuddy of The Reeks', for example, were on the guest list for the Muckross House gathering alongside Sir this and Lady that.

This was a moving reunion. Many of these families had only barely hung on to their grand houses. Others had left, but had eagerly come back for the occasion from the UK and further afield.

This gathering was inspired by a book *Voices from the Great Houses*, which contains memories of living in Castle Townshend, Cahernane, The Reeks, Muckross, The Lake Hotel and many more. Written by historians, Jane and Maurice O'Keeffe, the book gives a unique glimpse into life in these old historic houses, with stories from surviving members of the Anglo-Irish and 'old Irish' families who lived, and in many cases still live, in them. They talk about their family histories, their links to the surrounding communities and the fascinating details of life in these houses.

(Opposite above)
Beaufort House, outside Killarney, Co. Kerry, is one of the houses featured in 'Voices from the Great Houses'.

Photograph:
Valerie O'Sullivan

(Opposite below)
The gardens of Muckross House, Killarney.

Photograph: Muckross House Research Library, Trustees of Muckross House (Killarney) Ltd.

Tom Denny, a descendant of the Denny family who have given their name to Tralee's grandest street, travelled to this gathering from Dorset, where he is a stained glass artist. The Dennys were the leading family in Tralee for over two centuries and once owned 29,000 acres surrounding the town, but 100 years had elapsed since they were "properly here," he said.

Tom had renewed acquaintance with Tralee historians in recent years, allowing access to the family archive. He feels strongly about his connection with north Kerry. "In the 17th, 18th and 19th centuries in Co. Kerry there were around a dozen families who intermarried. The Kerry gentry were notorious for all being cousins," he remarked.

Brigitte Shelswell-White of Bantry House said that the Whites had arrived in Ireland before the plantations (the confiscation of Irish property) and had bought their lands instead of being granted them. Her husband, Egerton, is interviewed in the book about his early memories, but sadly he passed away before the book was published. "I am here for the two of us," she said.

Stawell St Leger Heard, formerly of Kilbrittain in Co. Cork, left Ireland in the 1950's, but said he was always more of an Irishman and donned the Irish scarf at rugby matches.

Local Kerry gentry who attended this memorable gathering included the Hilliard, MacCarthy-O'Leary and O'Connell families – the latter relatives of the Great Liberator, Daniel O'Connell.

It was a touching event, recalling people and places that have played a major role in our history.

Anne Lucey is a journalist and writer based in the South West.

Top of the World-Kelly gathering on the Galtees.

Photograph: Bridget Kelly

A Gathering of Gatherers -the launch of The Gathering.

Photograph: Jason Clarke

HWH Bunclody v Central Coast Sydney in a special gathering charity match.

Photograph: Joe Guinan

GAA / THE GATHERING

Seán Moran

The best story to illuminate the traditional reach of Gaelic games for the Irish diaspora and those unavoidably abroad remains the closing anecdote in Breandán Ó hEithir's sparkling memoir, *Over the Bar: A Personal Relationship with the GAA*, published in the centenary year of the Gaelic Athletic Association in 1984.

Bill Doonan was a settled Traveller who trained as a radio operator with the Army. During the Second World War, in search of adventure, he deserted and enlisted in the British army. In the autumn of 1943, during a lull in the Battle of Monte Cassino in southern Italy, he went missing from his unit.

A search revealed him up a tree on the side of a steep hill, apparently in a trance. In the midst of everything, Doonan – who would go on to win All-Ireland medals with Cavan in 1947 and 1948 – had found a vantage point where he could tune in his equipment in order to hear commentary on the second half of the All-Ireland football final between Cavan and Roscommon.

Over the Bar concludes with this paragraph: "If anyone ever asks you what the GAA is all about just think of Bill Doonan, the wanderer, on the side of that hill, in the middle of a World War – at home."

Seventy years on, modern travel and communications technology have made the connection with home a less complicated affair, and inter-county players – never mind supporters – can travel backwards and forwards for matches or access matches on the internet.

In this year of *The Gathering*, the Tipperary county board organised two events for expatriates who had been involved with the GAA in the county. It was a two-part get-together over a Saturday and Sunday of 100 people from the US, Canada, Australia and the UK. There was a traditional music concert on the Saturday night, and on the Sunday visitors attended the Limerick-Tipperary Munster championship match as guests of the county board and were invited to dinner afterwards.

All that was missing was the one thing Tipp officials couldn't organise. "The result (of the match) of course was a disappointment," according to Ger Ryan, the PRO of the Tipperary county board. "But everyone enjoyed the weekend, nonetheless."

The relative ease with which expatriates can maintain contact with the GAA at home is a recent blessing. The past was different. Home to Irish people in the last century was very often not where they lived, and keeping in touch was difficult. The mail boats and their connecting trains steamed back and forth bringing cargoes of unhappy exiles in one direction, and their often heartbroken letters in the other.

A single statistic will suffice to tell the scale of that story. Of every five children born in Ireland between 1931 and 1941, four would emigrate in the 1950's. It's one of the relatively unsung aspects of the GAA that in organising overseas it did so much to ease the misery of economic migrants, ordinary people who found themselves in a strange place through little choice of their own.

It's probably overly sentimental to emphasise the unhappy emigrant experience, because presumably there was also life and hope and just getting on with things. As Séamus J. King put it in his book, *The Clash of the Ash in Foreign Fields: Hurling Abroad*, talking about the GAA in London in the 1950's: "It was easy enough to get a team together. All that was necessary was to stand outside a Catholic Church on Sunday morning. And it was possible to get not only a team but an army of supporters also."

Tommy Harrell, the former long-serving secretary of the London county board, once outlined the central role the GAA played in facilitating emigrants: "The GAA introduces people to work and accommodation. People meet their wives and their husbands through the GAA over here. If you fall on hard times, the GAA has funds to help you out. I go home every year and I hear people talking about the GAA as a sports organisation and a cultural organisation. For emigrants, for people like us who have come away, it is those things but it's a welfare network as well."

Considering the year that's in it, the same London GAA would also become part of a most timely homecoming. On 26th May 2013, the London footballers recorded their first win in the senior championship since 1977 and earned a Connacht semi-final place against Leitrim in Carrick-on-Shannon. They beat them to contest the final against Mayo on July 21st, which they lost.

In May, Mark Gottsche was announced as the first London footballer to win a GAA/GPA Player of the Month award. He was born in Kellinghusen, Germany, and reared by his German dad and Irish mother in Galway, for whom he played at under-21 and briefly senior level. Having emigrated to London three years ago, he played a starring role in the historic victory over Sligo.

As a development officer for the GAA in London, Gottsche is helping spread the word of Gaelic games beyond Ireland. "We have about 14 or 15 under-age clubs in London and every club has three defined feeder schools. I remember coaching a Polish kid last year and he couldn't understand how they didn't have Gaelic football in Poland. He said, 'This is the best game ever, way better than soccer' ".

In its way, the perfect modern example of the GAA's global reach.

Seán Moran is GAA correspondent with The Irish Times.

2013 Connacht GAA Football Senior Championship Final, Mayo v London, Castlebar, Co. Mayo.

Photograph: Stephen McCarthy / Sportsfile

In a special gathering dubbed 'Oxbridge', thousands of spectators watched Muckross Rowing Club, Killarney, beat the world's most coveted rivals Oxford and Cambridge Boat Clubs, in a challenge race for the 'Lakes of Killarney Salters Cup'.

Photograph: Valerie O'Sullivan

MY TWO GREAT LOVES
A *reflection* by Loretta Brennan Glucksman

Loretta Brennan Glucksman chaired the American Ireland Fund for 18 years.

I was already in my 40s when I met the two great loves of my life. The first was my husband, Lewis Glucksman, and the second was Ireland.

Even though I didn't visit Ireland until I was older, my heart was there from the day I was born. I always had Irish blood flowing through my veins, being the granddaughter on my mother's side of a McHugh, (a coalminer), and a Murray from Leitrim; and on my father's side a Brennan from Donegal. I grew up in an Irish neighbourhood in Allentown, Pennsylvania, and had lots of Irish cousins. My grandfather Brennan lived next door and he taught me to pray in Irish.

In those days money was scarce and there was never any question of going to Ireland, which would have been like going to the moon. So it took my husband, a Hungarian-Jewish-American Wall Street investment banker, then CEO and Chairman of Lehman Brothers, to get me there.

Lew served in the US Navy during the Second World War. He spent his leave time in Ireland and developed a passion for the country, especially Irish writers. He first brought me in 1985, and I was smitten from the outset. I really felt I was home. That started a long connection with Ireland which continues to this day.

This connection eventually led to my involvement with the American Ireland Fund, which has raised $450 million for Irish causes over 30-plus years. This money has gone to education; arts and culture; peace and reconciliation; and community development. I am stepping down after 18 years as chairman and feel privileged to have served in this role.

In America in the late 1980's it was striking to Lew and me that New York University had lots of ethnic houses on campus, but there was no Irish house, so we decided to correct that. In 1993 we opened Glucksman Ireland House, with an Irish cultural centre which has gone from strength to strength.

Over the last 30 years I have been proud to have contributed to Irish life, serving on many Irish boards, including the IDA, Cork Airport Authority, the National Gallery, National Concert Hall, Trinity College, The Abbey Theatre, The National Library, The Royal College of Surgeons, University College Cork, and the University of Limerick. These are all organisations I care about, and I have learned so much from my involvement with them and have met so many great Irish people.

There is a very strong pull between Ireland and people all over the world, even those with no direct Irish lineage. What is crucial is that we respond to this and acknowledge that there is something important here to be nurtured. Whether it is Séamus Heaney's words, Gabriel Byrne's acting, or Colum McCann's stories, the Irish speak to and unite the world.

There is something in the Irish that will not be beaten. They will always bounce back. Maybe Ireland's resilience goes back to never being conquered by the Romans! We don't carry any of that baggage and that is why we have an independent spirit. People like to be associated with that spirit. People want to know Irish people and to connect with that energy.

When I came to Ireland first, people were sensible and didn't flash money and possessions around, but then things got more flamboyant and people lost the run of themselves, which was so un-Irish.

The recent financial crisis has been very hard for the country. Ireland just got on with it, and we are seeing light at the end of the tunnel. The government made the hard decisions that were needed – but it is especially the good, solid, ordinary people of Ireland who rallied so that the country could get through this. It is these people who are the backbone of Ireland.

Lew was diagnosed with terminal cancer in 2000 and was given six months to live, so we moved to Ireland to a house overlooking the sea near Cobh in Co. Cork, where he wanted to spend his last days. Thankfully, he survived six more years, and I give Ireland credit for extending his life. He was so happy there.

The staff in the local hospice during that time were amazing. They saved my life. They were there for me and Lew to reassure and comfort and advise us. They brought calmness, and Lew loved them all, joking and laughing when they came to care for him. Thanks to the hospice, Lew ended his days in peace, at home, and was fully alert to the last. He was meant to end his life in the place that he loved so well.

Lew was cremated; some of his ashes are scattered off the coast of Cork and the rest in our home in upstate New York, so I feel he is with me when I am in Ireland and the US. He is never far away. And for me, Ireland is where my heart is and always will be.

The sea front at Cobh.

Photograph: Fáilte Ireland

SAIL HOME TO YOUR ROOTS

It was a voyage that started in Liverpool and ended in Dublin. Sixteen novice sailors, including some descended from Irish emigrants, boarded two tall ships and embarked on a five-day journey across the Irish Sea as part of the *Sail Home to Your Roots Gathering*.

On their arrival into the Dublin docklands, they were greeted by friends and family as well as a number of dignitaries. The crews spent the weekend enjoying the fun and frolics of the Dublin Docklands Festival.

The event was all thanks to the partnership of Sail Training Ireland and Liverpool-based Merseyside Adventure Sailing Trust. It was also a precursor to a bigger get-together over the June Bank Holiday weekend, when the ships were joined by even larger Class A tall ships and another Class B vessel as part of the Dublin Port River Festival.

Some of the tall ships that sailed across the Irish Sea as part of The Gathering.

(Opposite)
Photograph: Michael Byrne

(Above)
Photograph: Chris Bacon

Photographs:
Alan Betson / The Irish Times,
Bryan O'Brien / The Irish Times,
Magdalena A. Golden,
Malcolm Mc Gettigan /
BigOMedia

Clara Glynn at the Explore the Shore Beach Safari in Salthill, Galway which was part of the Gathering Galway Sea Festival.

Photograph: Andrew Downes

IRELAND'S GOODWILL AMBASSADORS

A reflection by Marian Finucane

Marian Finucane presents The Marian Finucane Show on RTE Radio 1.

Citizen of the world, citizen of Europe, citizen of Ireland – I'm comfortable with all, but in the context of *The Gathering*, it's the Irish one that gets examination. Irishness and the significance it merits in the context of emigration. Its meaning is not something one contemplates regularly, yet for the tens of millions of people worldwide who claim it as their roots and identity, it clearly means a lot.

I remember, on a beautiful New York summery day, taking the ferry for a visit to Ellis Island, the point of entry for immigrants to the US. I tried to imagine myself in the place of all those people who had survived the passage from Ireland, their first sighting of the Statue of Liberty, the queuing up with fear and hope at the immigrant inspection centre, to be vetted for acceptance in the New World.

Some would not pass the medical and would be refused. Those that passed – and the numbers were staggering – were largely destitute.

Twelve million immigrants of all nationalities entered America through Ellis Island. The descendants of those immigrants make up nearly half the population of America now, and among them are the tens of millions who retained their Irish identity, changing to become not just Americans, but Irish Americans.

This is mirrored all over the world.

What stayed with me after that visit was how ill-equipped our emigrants were. Using the search facilities at Ellis Island on the Irish, I found Irish woman after woman described as 'servant girl', and Irish man after man as 'unskilled labourer'. I looked, with a tinge of envy on their behalf, at the English and Italian entries. Some of these had trades – a seamstress, a stone mason – but I did not find, in the searches I chose to make, any single mention of a skill or education attributed to an Irish entry. The entire visit was deeply moving, and saddening, and yet it represented hope and promise, a new life, a new world. These people were, and still are, connected to Ireland.

Nearly all my father's siblings emigrated. They were also unskilled, with just a basic National School education. That was in the 1930's. Then we had the waves of emigration in the 1950's and in the 1980's, and here we are yet again failing to provide for our current young adults whom we are exporting in tens of thousands. We have to feel some sense of anger at our failure, yet remarkably, those whom we failed for centuries have been loyal to us in Ireland and have largely served us well, retaining their identity with pride in their Irishness. One hears little bitterness.

Plus ça change… However, some things have changed, a little. Today's emigrants are educated, articulate and confident. Skype, What's App and so on have transformed contact with home. Flights are more affordable. What in the past was permanent exile is redefined as opportunity and adventure, but there is still loss for parents and inevitable moments of loneliness for those who leave.

We had a gathering on the radio programme with five 20-somethings home for Christmas 2012 from Vancouver, Berlin, Perth, London and Boston. Previously unacquainted, they developed an immediate affinity with one another, exchanging stories of living as an Irish person abroad. Firstly, each of them immediately felt welcomed in their country of choice, just because of where they came from. They had all become more conscious of their nationality when abroad:

"We all become more Irish when we are away…"
"We all speak a bit of Irish…"
"When you meet other Irish people you make an instant connection…"
"We have the same sense of humour!"

Individually and collectively they wanted to project a positive image of Ireland abroad. In fact, some really spoke with passion of their commitment to be the best ambassadors possible for this country. They recounted remarkably similar reactions from their new host countries, reflecting an expectation of Irish people of congeniality, generosity, hard work and humour; a belief that Irish people are steeped in the arts, literature and music, with a calling card of emotional intelligence.

What? Every one of us? While this is all very flattering, you might wonder how the myth arose. Irish people are fairly similar to all other peoples, largely decent, but, along with our saints and scholars, we have produced our fair share of charlatans and chancers! Ask the Irish at home, particularly around now, and you might get a different version of our identity to that which you will find abroad. However, overseas, generations of emigrants have done an excellent PR job for us. Separately, across Africa, the missionaries repeated the story and left a legacy of goodwill in country after country towards those who show up with a harp on their passport, even if people haven't a clue where this little Celtic dot is on the world map.

Let's be thankful for the myth and be aware of the debt we owe to all those millions of goodwill ambassadors. *The Gathering* is about these people. How we go about it will, I hope, draw on our best characteristics rather than our crass ones. We might remember that this good story for us is based on a deeply sad story repeated millions of times over. The diaspora was born of tears and loss over three centuries, reflecting political and economic failure. We have a lot to be grateful for from our diaspora.

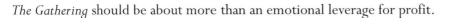

The official website refers to all the positive aspects of this. It also reminds us of the doom and gloom of our economic collapse and how this *Gathering* will help local industries. It undoubtedly can, but we should be careful about this.

The Gathering should be about more than an emotional leverage for profit.

Irish emigrants arriving at Ellis Island.

Photograph: The Irish Times

The conductor's shadow can still lead the choir! Captured at the Cork International Choral Festival's Choral Gathering Trail.

Photograph: Sarah Scanlon

GATHERING VOICES

Áine Kavanagh

As gatherings go, choral gatherings tick all the boxes.

Choirs are made up of all sorts of talented, motivated people. The kind who don't just gather to sing. They gather to tidy their town. They gather to support their footballers. They gather to grieve lost members of the community. They gather to celebrate local victories. They gather to entertain the parish each Christmas Eve, and every Saturday evening in between.

Choirs like to travel, and do so in great numbers. They take up almost the entire departure lounge of a small airport. They make friends with fellow choirs in faraway places. They establish long-lasting relationships that lead to invitations to perform in churches and theatres, in town halls and parks, in places we've never even heard of.

Choirs love to perform. They love an audience. They draw a crowd, entertain and soothe. They make us wish we could sing like them, so that we too could join a choir and travel the globe, bringing sweet harmony to our own community and communities of the world.

The Dunboyne Consort has been entertaining the people of Dunboyne for almost 40 years. Their annual performance of the *Hallelujah Chorus* from Handel's *Messiah* at Midnight Mass on Christmas Eve is a long-established tradition, along with that anxiety-inducing high note in *Oh, Holy Night*, and the fact that Midnight Mass is actually at eight o'clock. It's the recessional hymn that keeps everyone in their pew until the last *Hallelujah* has rung out. A split second of stunned silence is followed by rapturous applause, and everyone leaves the church on a high, invigorated by the powerful harmonies and the heart-warming feeling that now, it's Christmas.

This annual performance of the *Hallelujah Chorus* is something that those of us who have left Dunboyne — whether it's to go just up the road or further afield to America, Australia, Dubai or China — associate with 'home'. So, the Consort holds a special little place in all of our hearts. But little did we know they'd made such an impact on the sunny Côte d'Azur.

Director of the Dunboyne Consort, Dermot Brophy explained the very Irish 'French Connection': "A French acquaintance of mine in the Alliance Française in Dublin mentioned, in passing, that her mother was a member of a choir in a town near Nice. My ears pricked up and I immediately wondered if this choir might like to take part in an exchange. Within a matter of weeks, it was all arranged."

The choirs of Gattieres and St Etienne de Tiné received the Dunboyne Consort in the summer of 2012. The Meath delegation entertained the people of Nice at a series of performances, and their French hosts eagerly accepted the invitation to return for a special choral gathering, bringing an entourage of wives, husbands and supporters with them to Ireland in the spring of 2013.

Many arrived a full two weeks ahead of their performances to explore Ireland, a place they had never been to but had often dreamed of visiting. They travelled down the west coast, taking in the lakes of Connemara, immortalised by French singer, Michel Sardou, who penned the 1981 French hit, *Les Lacs du Connemara*.

In Dublin, they serenaded the then Lord Mayor, Naoise Ó Muirí, at the Mansion House. They visited the Book of Kells and the former House of Lords in College Green.

The visitors were particularly impressed by the warm welcome they received along the way. Christine Ricchiardi, soprano, joined the choir "just for fun." "It is a great way to see the world. I have been to Russia, to Corsica, but Ireland is really very beautiful," she explained.

The cuisine — and the Irish policy of offering tea and biscuits — was a hit too: "We ate very well in Ireland. We loved the fresh salmon, the seafood, fish and chips, drinking tea and eating biscuits all day!"

Jean-Luc and Jean-Georges faithfully accompanied their wives on the trip. They took hundreds of photographs and were suitably captivated by their first visit to Ireland. "The people are so welcoming. Since we arrived, everywhere we've gone, we have been very well received."

François Jeanneqin, a retired English teacher, was given the daunting task of presenting the French choir's performances to their audience at Dunboyne's GAA clubhouse. He rose to the challenge with aplomb, enjoying the spotlight and the opportunity to showcase typical French wit, referencing Munster's defeat to Clermont in the Heineken Cup Semi-Final: "Ladies and gentlemen, it is a great pleasure and a great honour to be with you this evening. Especially on this evening when you let us win."

Both choirs shared the task of entertaining the local crowd with a series of songs in French and English, culminating in a joint performance of *Down by the Salley Gardens*.

François said taking part in this gathering was a truly moving experience. "We have felt a strong sense of sharing and belonging. In fact, we enjoyed it so much, we are even thinking of staying!"

They left, 'ecstatic', the following day, but there is no doubt they will return. "My inbox is overflowing with superlatives," explained Brophy in the wake of their departure. "Maybe it was just the heat of the afterglow, but they all said 'we must return to Ireland next year'. You know, they really had a ball."

Áine Kavanagh, who is from Dunboyne, is currently the PR manager with The Gathering Ireland 2013.

The choirs of Gattieres and Saint Etienne de Tiné performing at the Mansion House, Dublin.

Pictured at the Town of 1000 Beards Gathering in Ballymoe, Co. Galway are clockwise from left Tom Flynn, Pat Diskin, Martin Costelloe, Tom Waldron and John Griffin.

Photograph: Andrew Downes

COMING HOME

A reflection by Colum McCann

Colum McCann is an award-winning Irish writer, based in New York.

There is a priceless copy of James Joyce's *Ulysses* in the New York Public Library. A first edition. Signed by Joyce to his friend James Stephens.

The collision of book and place is sacred. The library is probably the finest in the world. So too, of course, is the book: the most acclaimed novel of the 20th century. So when I had a chance to see the copy in the winter of 2011, I immediately said yes. I got on the subway. Got off at 42nd Street. Walked along Fifth Avenue in the slush. Shook out my umbrella. Walked up the steps, past the famous lion statues, into the library. Up to the third floor. Into a rare book room where the curators greeted me warmly.

The book was laid out on a piece of blue velvet, opened carefully and methodically. The curators wore gloves. They treated the book with proper awe. I was supervised every moment of the way. I didn't even get to touch the pages. I leaned over the book, breathed the phrases in. *The ineluctable modality of the visible.*

Part of the charm of books, of course, is that they disintegrate. Although the language lasts forever   in both a digital and imaginative sense – no book can be protected forever. There are simple laws of nature. Even if we sealed our books in hermetic tombs, some distant day entropy will gnaw at the pages. It's called age – it's the most democratic thing in the world and it happens to the best of us, even Joyce.

So when the book was carefully closed and lifted to be put away, a tiny flake of page fell from inside onto the blue cloth beneath. This happens. That's life. Books will flake. It was just a crumb, really. Slightly smaller than a thumbtack. It sat on the blue felt cloth. The library staff didn't notice it. They took the book away. To be wrapped, protected, properly humidified. But the flake still lay there on the cloth. I stared at it. It would soon become dust.

I got ready to leave. Unhooked my jacket from the back of the chair. Thought about it again. Looked down at the flake of *Ulysses*.

And then I did what anyone with a fondness for Joyce would: I licked my thumb, picked up the crumb, and ate it. Or rather let it dissolve slowly.

The book that I return to, when I return to Ireland, is always *Ulysses*. I make no apology for this. I don't find it pretentious. I don't think it's overwrought. Nor do I believe that it's an impossible read. Sure, it is difficult, but all worthy things are, in their own way, difficult.

It's just a good book. I like it. It makes me laugh. It puzzles me. It confounds me. It frustrates me. It thrills me. I find it worth reading. That's enough.

And literature lives on in the most peculiar ways. The messy layers of human experience get ordered and reordered by what we take into our minds, our memories, our imaginations. Books can carry us to the furthest side of our desires. We can travel, we can remain, or we can hide in plain sight. And sometimes they mean so much more than just the physical or even the imaginative object.

Early in 2013 I lost my best friend. Brendan Bourke. A photographer, a filmmaker, a writer, a teacher. He had struggled with his health for many years, but somehow he had always managed to bring a spark to whatever life gathered around him, including his own.

Brendan knew of my obsession with *Ulysses* and he promised that, one day, he would read it. I tried to encourage him to read the more salacious parts of Molly's soliloquy, or to begin with Bloom at breakfast, or to sit for a while with the Citizen in Little Britain Street. He could even read the novel backwards if he wanted to. I was fairly sure he would enjoy it, once he got over its supposed difficulty. Bren was a Dubliner after all. And he was a good reader. And *Ulysses* – despite the aura that somehow gathers around it – was the perfect Dublin novel.

He never read the book, however. He talked about it, but never read it. Life got in the way. There was always some new film project that overtook the task. Or a photograph to take. Or another surgical procedure to undergo. He was always just *about* to read it. *Good puzzle to cross Dublin without passing a pub*. We once sat in the Stag's Head together and tried to figure out if there was a way. The novel was at the cusp for Brendan: he was always about to embark on it. After his brother Kyron gave him his kidney – and almost four more years of life – he said he was going to finally sit down and read it. It became one of his ambitions. That, and race a rally car. That, and finish a film of ours: *As If There Were Trees*. That, and bring his partner Liz on a journey to the States. That, and so many other things.

Brendan died early in the New Year. His body failed him. He was young, or young enough, at 50, to make me think that it was entirely wrong. I flew home to Dublin from New York. The next day I talked with Liz. She was going through his things in preparation for the funeral. Brendan had, she said, purchased a copy of *Ulysses* just before Christmas. She knew because she had found it among his Christmas things, with a receipt from Hodges Figgis stuck inside. She could tell from the spine that he had not yet cracked the book open. It made her smile, though, to think about it. He had, at least, bought it. He was ready for it.

The next day, she took the copy and placed it on Brendan's chest in the open wicker coffin that he lay inside, in the funeral home in Fairview. It was her gesture to him to carry the story with him.

I have never liked the idea of an open coffin, but later that evening I got the chance to sit in the funeral home before the viewing. Brendan was laid out in the open coffin, dressed in his favourite cowboy boots and a paisley shirt. The copy of *Ulysses* lay slap bang in the middle of his chest, just above his folded hands. Still uncracked, unopened.

I had about a half hour to spend with him, alone, before others came in. I pulled up a chair and sat beside him.

One of Brendan's favourite lines from my own short stories: *Well fuck it anyway, we really need some new blood in midfield*.

And so I did, again, what anyone would do. I picked up the book and began to read.

Death takes away a lot of things, but it can't ever take away our stories. This is the beauty of literature. Stories don't die with us. They live on on. Literature is, in a very pure sense, the place where we learn to remain alive.

I do not know what page that solitary crumb fell from when I visited the New York Public Library. Who knows what chapter of *Ulysses* it came from? Who knows what might have become of it – thrown in the rubbish, or swept away, or maybe even kept in a plastic bag by one of the librarians to be cherished. It hardly matters. It is long gone. I ate it. Fair enough.

And while I don't know what might have happened to that flake of paper if I had left it there, I do know what I read to Brendan Bourke when I sat with him in the funeral home in Fairview, and perhaps part of it belonged to that flake. I leaned over the coffin and picked the book from off his chest. I opened it up and went straight to the *What is a nation?* section, where Bloom argues with the Citizen. *Ireland*, said Bloom, *I was born here, Ireland.*

The time ticked away, as time does. But I wanted a little more for him, my pal. So I sat by Brendan's coffin and flicked forward in the book and read to him the filthiest, naughiest, dirtiest, most wonderful parts of Molly's soliloquy. To give him a bit of a smile for the beyond. To send him off with a laugh.

Just imagine that. To die with a laugh.

Brendan Bourke

Former Taoiseach Liam Cosgrave and Morgan Campbell, a 2nd year student at CBS James Street, pictured at a gathering of staff and pupils of three schools in Basin Lane, Dublin 8. Mr Cosgrave's father, W.T. Cosgrave, attended CBS James Street.

Photograph: Alan Betson / The Irish Times

THE POWER CLAN GATHERING

Anne Power

Here in Waterford, the surname Power is four times more common than any other, and, being a Power and a native of the city, it would have been considered traitorous of me not to attend one of the biggest family clan gatherings in the country.

This ancient family name descends from Sir Robert De Poer, who, it is said, came to Ireland with Strongbow in 1172 AD. In that year, King Henry II granted by charter to Robert De Poer the City of Waterford and "the whole province thereabouts", and made him Marshal of Ireland. The Power family had what they considered their own 'country' and enforced their own levies.

The Power clan gathering was marked by guided walks filled with history, flora and fauna, Irish music and dance, horse racing, genealogy talks, battle re-enactments, family gatherings and much more. Powers from across the city and county gathered, along with many descendants from the UK, Canada, Newfoundland and further afield.

I joined the '*Hurtle Trail Walk*' with expert tour guide, Ray McGrath, on Saturday morning. We gathered at the school above Cheekpoint and walked the route which is part of the '*Emigrant Trail*' along the banks of the beautiful River Suir. Ray, a historian and also Chair of the Irish Wildlife Trust, guided us along the stunning trail, which links the villages of Cheekpoint and Passage East, and offers breathtaking views of the Suir estuary, which was key to the growth of Waterford and the Power family.

(Opposite)
A Power from old - one of the characters who took part in the Power Clan Gathering.

Photograph: Joe Evans

Ray told us that the River Suir from Waterford to Dunmore East – a 16-mile stretch – is synonymous with the history of Ireland and the various invasions and settlements. The Suir has seen many battles over the years, one of them involving the Power clan against the Mayor of Waterford. In 1368, the Powers of Waterford of Dunhill wanted to control elements of the Waterford City Council. Lord Dunhill, Robert Power, established an alliance with the O'Driscoll Clan in west Cork. In due course the Powers and the O'Driscolls sailed up the river to do battle. When the Mayor of Waterford heard about it he got three ships together and sailed down to meet them and the battle was fought. The Mayor and Robert Power were killed, and shortly afterwards that line of the Powers died out.

Another battle took place between the citizens of Waterford and the combined forces of the Powers and the O'Driscolls almost 100 years later. In 1461 the then Mayor of Waterford organised an expedition to go and do battle at the home of the O'Driscolls in west Cork. The city captured three galleys belonging to the enemy and sailed back to Waterford. Ever since, the emblem of Waterford has been three ships to commemorate this event.

As part of the gathering a memorable re-enactment of the Power and O'Driscoll battle with the city forces took place on Tramore Beach.

In all, the weekend was a wonderful journey through the history of Waterford and the Power family, with *craic agus ceoil* and an all too rare opportunity to meet lots of old and new friends and family.

Anne Power is from Tramore and is director of Powerhouse PR, based in the South East.

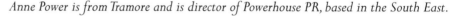

Kate Power, Shannon and Roisín Murphy and Iarla Hennessy re-enacting traditional ways of life.

Photograph: Noel Browne

A Power struggle.

Photograph: Joe Evans

The huge crowd including lots of overseas visitors pictured as they made their way to Dunhill Castle during the Power Clan Gathering.

Photograph: Noel Browne

Photographs:
Alan Betson / The Irish Times,
Brenda Fitzsimons / The Irish Times,
Don MacMonagle,
Malcolm McGettigan / BigOMedia

Photograph: Alan Betson /
The Irish Times

BEING IRISH
A reflection by Pat Shortt

Pat Shortt is one of Ireland's top comedians.

If there is ever a competition for the most stereotypical, quintessential Irish upbringing on the planet I reckon I'll at least make it into the knockout stages. My first name is Patrick, I was born in Thurles, in Co. Tipperary in the 1960's and by the time my parents had finished procreating there were 11 of us. Our household was headed by a primary school principal with a love of everything Irish, a man who did his level best to hand it on to us. He was a *gaelgoir,* played Irish music and had an abiding interest in tradition, culture and history.

From my earliest years everything around me confirmed, affirmed and suggested that I was a product of Paddy's Green Shamrock Shore - maybe not quite a product of the shore but certainly a product of the green interior.

As soon as I was able to put my nose outside our front door in Thurles my senses were assaulted by the sights, sounds, smells, tastes and touches that made the Ireland of the time. In fact Thurles was like Ireland in concentrate. Surrounded by farmers it was home to an archbishop, a cathedral, two seminaries, two major convent boarding schools, a sugar factory and Semple Stadium, the spiritual home of the GAA. You could say I was brought up on a mixed diet of beet, blessings and beating Cork.

To paraphrase Eamon Kelly, in the Thurles of my youth you couldn't throw a stone without rising a lump on the head of an archbishop, priest, trainee priest or nun.

I suppose I had the ideal childhood for the great Irish novel. If only I had a bit more hardship and oppression I'd be the toast of the literati and a regular guest on these earnest, late night arts programmes where I'd be expected to furrow my brow and grunt. The only memory I have of oppression is being chased with my friends out of the handball alleys of St Patrick's College and the Palatine seminary.

On the face of it, a town like Thurles was characterised by sanctity and sanctimoniousness but on the flip side there existed a world of sacrilege, madness and irreverent hilarity. The place gave me the raw materials and the tools for a trade that has provided me with a good living since I fell on to the stage with Jon Kenny more than 25 years ago. The secret of our success together and my success as a solo artist is found in a knack for recognising and tapping into the acceptable level of madness that is part of every Irish community.

As a comic actor and a clown I reflect back to people the madness and hilarity that is their every day life. We Irish have a huge capacity to laugh at ourselves and when I'm on stage the loudest and longest laughs are raised when people recognise themselves, the things they say and the things they do in the anecdotes I act out and the turns of phrase I use. Take, for instance, the image of the lads eating their dinner at half eight on the morning of the big match "in order to get a good run at the day"; this always brings the house down because people have memories of eating the dinner at eleven o'clock on the morning of a big match. I just push it back about two and a half hours and we all recognise the madness in it.

In that regard, I don't play on the negative for comedy, I play on the everyday and while it causes belly laughter it also gives rise to many a wry smile.

I work in comedy with raw materials that include madness and chaos but this does not mean my life is mad and chaotic. A capacity for hard work and good business are as much part of being Irish as artistic talents.

Times are tougher now, audiences are smaller, sell-outs are more difficult and long runs don't happen as easily. However, my product is me and I still believe in that product. I work as hard at developing and promoting it as if I started yesterday.

I'm busy but I'll also be found washing glasses in my pub in Castlemartyr. It's all part of what I am and being Irish has made it all possible.

Some of the 285 Limerick locals who broke the World Record for the most people dressed as Saint Patrick gathered in one place.

Photograph: Seán Curtin

THE GATHERING OF STONES
Rebecca Kelly

I've heard it said on more than one occasion that the memories and voices of the past are entombed within stone. If this is true, the stones that made up the old immigrant docks near Battery Park in New York contain the imprints of the millions of people who passed over them across the centuries.

How many of them were Irish? What sort of lives awaited them? Did they ever get to see their native land again? We will never know, but one thing is certain – their footsteps will continue to echo across the Lough Boora Parklands in Co. Offaly, as some of those same stones now sit at the heart of a new monument, specially created to mark *The Gathering*.

The culmination of four days hard work, this new dry stone wall structure contains a number of elements. The outer circle is made up of four different sections, each representing the four provinces of Ireland, and each with its own specially chiselled emblem, while the inner section houses stones from New York in a cruciform shape, representing the diaspora.

Almost 40 stonemasons and stone carvers from all over the world, including Canada, America, Austria, Scotland, Wales and of course, Ireland, were part of the build. It was a proud moment for Tom Parkin, who made the journey all the way from Vancouver, Canada. "There's a great sense of pride in re-establishing this ancient craft. People want to be a part of it, and I think they will be bragging about this for many years to come."

Planning for *The Gathering of Stones* – a joint initiative between the Dry Stone Wall Association of Ireland (DSWAI) and the Stone Foundation in America – began in November

Dry Stone Wall Association of Ireland member Christian Helling carves the names of loved ones remembered.

Photograph: Paul James

2012, when Nick Aitken, a master craftsman from Scotland, contacted the DSWAI with the idea. An organising committee was soon set up and a plan was put in place not only to build the structure but also to invite people to 'bring a stone home'. Many did, including those involved in the build and members of the public. Some even shared moving stories while having them incorporated in memory of their loved ones.

The project then took on a whole new dimension with the donation of the New York stones by Bobby Watt, a master stonemason based in Ottawa, Canada. Bobby and his team had been asked to help with the restoration of the area between the Irish Famine memorial in Battery Park and 14th Street in New York in the autumn of 2001. However, following the events of 9/11, the project was delayed. Instead, the stones were extracted between the summers of 2002-2003 and taken to Canada. Following a call from Nick last year, Bobby was more than happy to help bring them to Lough Boora.

A renowned traditional singer, Bobby was so inspired by the idea that he wrote a song in honour of the occasion. Entitled *The Whispering of the Stones*, it's a poignant description of the voices contained within the stone.

> *Let's bring the stones home, boys, Lough Boora is shining.*
> *Bring the stones home to their rest*
> *Let's bring the stones home, boys, their spirits are pining.*
> *Bring the stones home from the West.*

A rendition by Donegal stonemason, Rónán Crehan, left many in tears at the end of an emotionally charged few days in the heart of Ireland. The profound effect of this structure was clear to see on the faces of those who built it. "I have to pinch myself," said Ken Curran, secretary of the DSWAI, "it's unbelievable to see our pipe dream come to life. Considering we didn't receive any funding, and with all the work done by volunteers, it's pretty spectacular what's been achieved here."

Rebecca Kelly is a freelance writer and broadcaster from Birr, Co. Offaly.

Photographs:
Gerry Dolan, Paul James
Sunny Weiler

The Tale of the Tongs is a commemoration to past generations of the mystical Inishturk Island off the Co. Mayo Coast. It forms part of Travis Price's Spirit of Place project, which was brought to Ireland as part of The Gathering.

Photograph: Michael McLaughlin

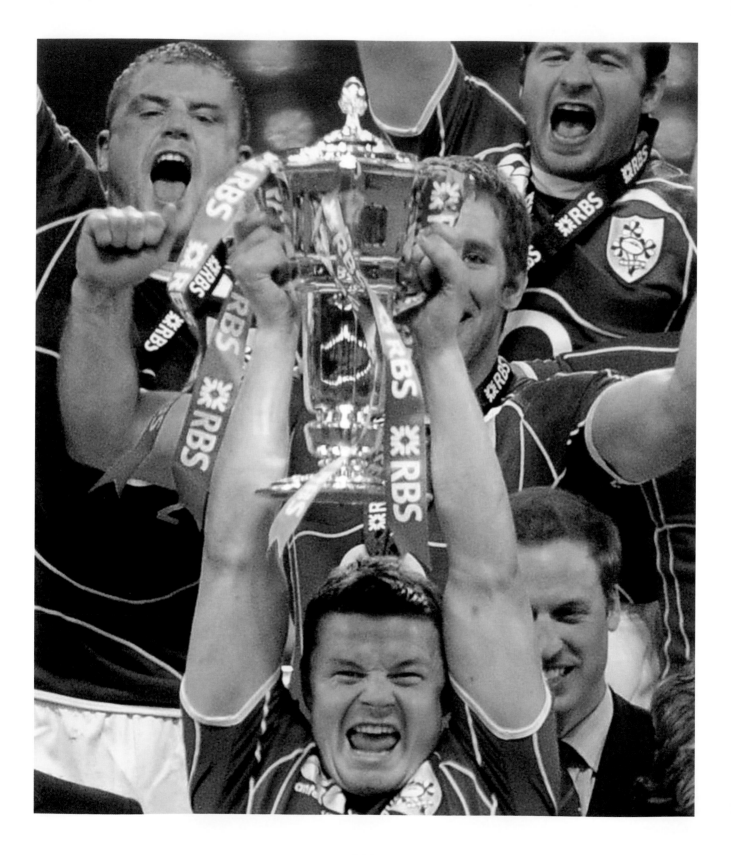

IMPOSSIBLE IS NOTHING

A reflection by Brian O'Driscoll

Brian O'Driscoll is one of the all-time greats of Irish rugby.

(Opposite)
Ireland captain Brian O'Driscoll lifts the RBS Six Nations Championship trophy in 2009 after defeating Wales to claim their first Grand Slam in 61 years.

Photograph: Stephen McCarthy / Sportsfile

I am a proud Irishman, fortunate to have represented my country in my chosen sport many times, on occasion as captain of the team. The pride I experience when I put on the green jersey and go into battle on the rugby field is as strong today as it was when it all began 14 years ago.

Ireland is a country which punches well above its weight and makes a massive impact on the world stage in music, in business, in the arts, and of course in sport. I feel so lucky and privileged to be part of that.

There are many, many things about wearing the green shirt that fill me with a sense of satisfaction and joy.

It is the pride taken in seeing the passion of those who follow us at home and abroad, hoping for victory, but always gracious and generous in defeat.

It is the knowledge that representing Ireland carries with it a tradition of never giving up, always striving harder and harder to succeed, and being there for your team-mates when they need you most.

It is knowing, despite the rough times our country has been going through, that my team-mates and I have been able to bring moments of hope and happiness to Irish people through some success on the rugby pitch.

I have been fortunate to have been part of cherished moments in Irish sport, not least in Cardiff in 2009, when we beat Wales to win our first Grand Slam in 61 years. On that day I felt a burden being lifted and a sense of unimaginable relief, as a country joyfully celebrated a triumph that had eluded it for so long. To have captained the side to victory made it even more special.

Another highlight was the 2011 World Cup in New Zealand, and meeting Irish fans working there. It was a real reminder to me of the impact of the recession and the fact that so many of our young people have had to look abroad for careers.

But we should not despair at the fact that thousands have left Ireland through emigration. Yes, it is tough for the families they have left behind. But we should also take the view that fine young Irish men and women are shining the Irish light in all corners of the globe. They are flying the green flag wherever they are, proud of their roots and never forgetting who they are and where they come from. This year of *The Gathering* is a great opportunity for them to celebrate their Irishness and hopefully get home to reconnect with family and friends.

At 34 years of age, I am well aware that I won't be part of special sporting moments for too much longer, at least not as a player on the pitch. The next phase of life, with all it has to offer, lies only around the corner, and you could find no better country in the world in which to bring up a family than Ireland.

One day soon, when my boots eventually get hung up, I will reflect on all the opportunities that have been presented to me in my career, and the debt of gratitude I owe to the people of Ireland for their loyalty and support.

For all our failings, I do believe that we have much to be proud of as a nation and in all that we have achieved. On and off the sports field, there is a determination to succeed and to deal with any problems thrown our way. To be born fighters is built into our psyche. In sport, this is called the 'winning mentality'. We need this in all walks of life, now more than ever.

Brian O'Driscoll offloads during the British and Irish Lions' 1st test against South Africa in 2009.

Photograph: Billy Stickland / INPHO

KENNEDY GATHERING
Seán Reidy

On 18th June, 2013 – a humid morning, with warm rain descending – I strolled up the avenue in Arlington Cemetery in Virginia towards the graveside of President John F. Kennedy. I noticed the figure of Congressman Joseph Kennedy, the latest in the long line of the Kennedy family to be elected to national office, coming towards me. He was accompanied by his wife, Lauren.

Following brief words of introduction, we walked together towards the graveside. Joseph is the most soft-spoken of the Kennedys that I have met, and I sensed a very gentle nature. There was a large crowd, including many from Wexford who had travelled over for the occasion. There, too, were Kennedy cousins: Timothy Shriver, President of the Special Olympics, and Sydney Lawford McKelvy.

We were there to take a light from the eternal flame at President Kennedy's graveside and bring it to New Ross as a gathering torch to light the Emigrant Flame beside the Famine Ship, Dunbrody, as part of the *JFK50* celebrations. This was to be a permanent flame of hope and inspiration to all Irish emigrants. And this journey of the torch would fulfil, at least symbolically, President Kennedy's promise, "to return to Ireland in the springtime."

The occasion was solemn, with a sombre hush invaded only by the rather intrusive presence of television cameras and journalists with microphones, looking for

(Opposite)
Seán Reidy, CEO of the JFK Trust, with Caroline Kennedy.

Photograph: Paddy Delaney

149

interviews. A colour party from the Irish Army was matched by a similar presence from the US defence forces, and a lone piper played a lament on the overseeing hillside. The Irish national anthem was sung by Michael Londra, and Anthony Kearns gave a stirring rendition of the *Star Spangled Banner*. I have never heard it better sung and the hairs stood on the back of my neck.

This was a special day. The Kennedy gathering had begun.

Forty members of the Kennedy family travelled to Ireland for what was surely the most iconic gathering of the year. The Kennedys are the closest Ireland and America come to having a royal family, and each branch of the family was represented: the Shrivers; the Lawfords; Robert Kennedy's family; Senator Edward Kennedy's family; Jean Kennedy Smith and her daughter; and of course, President Kennedy's daughter, Caroline, with her husband, Ed, and their children, Jack, Tatiana and Rose.

Preparations for the visit took months, and lots of work was done on infrastructure around the Kennedy legacy in Wexford in advance. A new visitor centre was completed at the Kennedy Homestead in Dunganstown; there was the re-dedication of the JFK Arboretum and the opening of a new Presidential exhibit there; and a new podium was sculpted to mark the very spot where President Kennedy spoke when he visited Ireland in 1963 at the Quayside in New Ross.

The *piece de résistance*, however, was the globe installed adjacent to the Dunbrody Famine Ship to house the Emigrant Flame.

In Dublin, the Kennedy influx started. Former Congressman, Patrick Kennedy, his wife, Amy, and their children, Owen and Harper, arrived, as did Caroline Kennedy and her family. They were followed by many more Kennedys including Kathleen Kennedy Townsend and her husband, David; Sydney Lawford McKelvy with her husband, Peter; Max Kennedy Jnr. and Chris Kennedy Jnr.

Max and Chris later asked where they might find a nice Irish pub, and I took them to Searsons in Baggot Street to experience some Dublin nightlife.

The torch arrived in Dublin Airport and was immediately transferred to the *MV Orla* for transport by sea to New Ross. The official *JFK50* exhibition was opened in the National Library, where we got our first glimpse of the new generation of Kennedys, as Caroline introduced her daughter, Tatiana, to speak on behalf of the family. There was an event at the US Ambassador's residence, with a surprise visit by President Higgins and his wife, Sabina, and then a State Banquet in Iveagh House.

The party began in earnest the next day in New Ross. The Kennedys were greeted on the quayside by the people of the town and their Irish cousins, the Grennans from Dunganstown. There was a tour of the Dunbrody Famine Ship, where the Kennedys learned what the journey was like for their ancestor, Patrick Kennedy, when he left Irish shores to make a new life in America back in 1848. Molly Kennedy said to me that the actors on the Dunbrody had made history come alive for the Kennedy children. There were seven children under the age of 14 in the travelling party, and they were joined by four Grennan cousins.

The Gala Homecoming Dinner in Brandon House gave the local community in New Ross an opportunity to welcome the Kennedys home. Kathleen Kennedy Townsend and Jean Kennedy Smith spoke here.

There was a lot of emotion when the new Visitor Centre in Dunganstown was officially opened by the Taoiseach. Caroline spoke, and Senator Ted Kennedy's grandchildren, Kiley and Grace, unveiled a bust of their grandfather. Séamus Heaney delivered an oration.

It was then on to the JFK Arboretum for the re-dedication and Max Jnr. and Chris Jnr. stepped forward to give a fascinating joint speech, another indication that the new

Spectators at the opening of the Kennedy Homestead and Visitor Centre.

Photograph: Eric Luke / The Irish Times

generation of Kennedys were emerging. Riley, aged 13, and his younger sister, Rowen – the children of Douglas Kennedy – were interviewed by a local radio station, and spoke clearly and with confidence.

And then to the New Ross Quayside for the final and most emotional event, the lighting of the eternal Emigrant Flame from the torch which arrived on the Navy vessel, *Orla*, with Jean Kennedy Smith on board.

Caroline Kennedy, Taoiseach Enda Kenny and Jean Kennedy Smith lit the Emigrant Flame from the three torches presented by the Special Olympic athletes. Judy Collins sang Amazing Grace; the Air Corp did a stunning flyover; and the grandson of President Kennedy, Jack Schlossberg, made his maiden speech on the same quayside that his grandfather had spoken from 50 years ago. The torch had surely been passed to the new generation of Kennedys.

The following day, a car pulled up outside the Dunbrody Famine Ship Visitor Centre, and an elegant elderly lady walked up to the Emigrant Flame and paused for a moment of quiet. It was Jean Kennedy Smith, surely reflecting on the visit with her brother 50 years previously. She too must have been proud that *The Gathering* had strengthened the link between the new generation of Irish and the Kennedys, ensuring that the flame of hope and inspiration that John F. Kennedy represented is kept alive and passed onto future generations.

Seán Reidy is the CEO of the JFK Trust.

(Left)
Taoiseach Enda Kenny, Jean Kennedy Smith and Caroline Kennedy, at the opening of the Kennedy Homestead and Visitor Centre.

Photograph: Eric Luke / The Irish Times

(Opposite)
JFK drinking tea in New Ross in 1963.

Photograph: The Irish Times

The runners and riders come through Joe's Water Splash first time around during the Fr Sean Breen Memorial Steeplechase during the Punchestown Gathering Festival.

Photograph: Donall Farmer / INPHO

Kylemore Abbey, Co. Galway

Photograph: Kylemore Tourism

DIFFERENT NARRATIVES; SAME LANDSCAPE

A reflection by Áine Lawlor

Áine Lawlor is a well-known broadcaster who co-presents Morning Ireland on RTE Radio 1.

Recently we travelled to Clonmel to lay the ashes of my late parents-in-law, Barclay and Dorothy, in their family plot.

It was a poignant journey, and a reminder of that first time we travelled that road all together, when Ian and I were first engaged. A lot of the route was familiar to me from family holidays in Kerry. To pass the time and stop squabbles, my mother would point out the fairy forts, the saints' wells and the mass rocks we passed – not just keeping the peace in the back seat, but also teaching us to read the history in the Irish landscape.

But sitting in the back seat with Barclay all those years ago, I heard a different landscape described. This was a land of Lord so-and-so's estate, of cricket grounds, of named families that lived in good houses. The same landscape, but different readings. It was the first time I'd seen the Irish countryside in split frame; the first time I understood the Southern echoes of the mantra John Hume was hammering out in the emerging peace process – two traditions, one land. Peace would be a deal between the two traditions about recognising difference and sharing the same land together.

Back then, I saw only the contrast in the ways my mother and my father-in-law read the countryside. But a love of gardens began to teach me more about the way both traditions lived together.

The first garden I loved was my grandmother's, where the plot had a practical purpose. The lovely old apple trees provided a winter's supply of apple jelly. There were potatoes, greens, onions, carrots and herbs; chickens and homemade wine. There was

157

the big turf pile outside too, but this was no romantic picture postcard, even though it was beautiful. It was the practical self-sufficiency of a family that had survived decades of tough times in the new Irish state.

In our own suburban home, we had vegetables too. However, we gave up growing them after Ireland joined the Common Market. The big argument that persuaded my mother to vote 'yes' was the promise of all those imported vegetables. I just thought that an end to hours of watering chores in the garden was a good idea, especially when you could be indoors watching *Kojak* or the *Late Late Show* on your family's new colour telly instead.

Modernity and free education — less obvious changes in Irish society, to the child I was then — brought me to Trinity, and to the man I was to marry, a man from a landowning, Protestant background. Through Ian, I learned stories about the sale of land and fine houses, and about the decline of Protestant wealth. Two narratives, one landscape. Those ruins we see as we drive on our new motorways, those medieval castles and round towers, tell such apparently different stories from the centuries-later ruins of the houses of the gentry. Most of us don't even notice that now. They are all part of the romance of the Irish landscape.

A few years ago, on holiday in Waterford, Ian and I escaped the kids and drove to Mount Congreve, the magnificent house and estate of the late Ambrose Congreve, still in private hands. We arrived at lunchtime, and ran straight into a mini traffic-jam on the long and narrow driveway — a puzzle in the middle of the back of beyond, until we realised that it was estate workers leaving for their break. This was a far cry from any other garden I had seen. It was an echo of centuries past: more than 70 acres of magnificent parkland on the banks of the River Suir, with a four-acre walled garden, lavishly planted and immaculately maintained. The scale of it was quietly stunning… 2,000 rhododendrons, 600 camellias, hundreds of rarities.

Most of the old gardens we had visited before had been lovely — but crumbling — affairs, faded beauties beyond the care of their ageing and less well-off owners. This was a wealthy plantsman's beautiful playground, but in all its beauty, it was a reminder of past divisions too.

Another holiday, another wonderful garden, this one in the capable hands of the Office of Public Works: Kylemore Abbey, a lush jewel stranded in Connemara's barren beauty. And the biggest surprise was the ruined hothouse where pineapples were grown in Victorian times. It was incongruous, pineapples in Connemara, and just a few decades after the Famine. As a gardener, I had to admire not just the Henrys of Manchester, who bought and commissioned this wonder, but also the skill and passion of the anonymous pineapple gardeners who had made those precious plants bear fruit. It takes more than money and heat to produce such an exotic fruit in that grey and rainy place, and I can only hope that those gardeners whose pride it was got to taste that fruit themselves.

Fruit was the theme I associate with another gardener, the late Dr Keith Lamb, whose midlands garden I visited one wintry afternoon a few years ago. Dr Lamb was old then, and ailing, but his garden in winter was still a treasure trove of rarities, even though many of these were underground, and he could only tell me their names. By now I knew that as an agricultural scientist back in the 1940's, he had recognised that old Irish varieties of apple tree were disappearing and could be lost forever, so he took on the task of tracking down as many of them as he could and saving them. Thanks to Keith Lamb, we can still grow apples like *Honey Ball, Greasy Pippin, Lady's Finger, Maiden's Blush* and *Widow's Friend*. These apples taste good and are well adapted to our climate; they add to genetic diversity, but besides all that, they tell the stories of the people who named them and bred them, and those who just minded and pruned them.

I don't know the names of the apples that grew in my grandmother's orchard, and anyway they are gone now, pulled out in the Celtic Tiger era, when the house was sold and refurbished. But I think it's a safe bet that her apples had names and stories.

There are stories of our split frame and intertwined histories, of what was shared and divided. What unites them all in the end is a love of the land they lived in.

McSHANE - FOX GATHERING
Sligo

It was a dream come true for 58 members of the McShane and Fox families when they came together for a family gathering not to be forgotten in Enniscrone, Co. Sligo. Relatives travelled from Philadelphia, Austin, Houston, England and Denmark for this special event.

The gathering began with a Mass at Enniscrone church, and from there on to the Ocean Sands Hotel for dinner. The big surprise of the evening was the appearance of the band, The Strawboys, whose lead singer is a family cousin.

Dancing with the Strawboys.

Photograph: John Fox

LEE GATHERING
Donegal

Mossy surrounded by some family members.

Forty-five members of the Lee family congregated in Bundoran, Co. Donegal for a gathering not to be forgotten.

There were speeches, monologues and songs as relatives from Canada, Boston, London, Dublin, Galway and Donegal came together to reminisce and swap stories. It was all organised by Morris 'Mossy' Lee who was unable to join the festivities after coming down with pneumonia two weeks before. But when Mohammed can't come to the mountain, the mountain came to Mohammed — so instead some of the group paid him a visit in the hospital. He was thrilled to see them all and it lifted his spirits no end.

(Top)
Photograph: Thomas Gallagher

Sadly Mossy passed away on July 1st 2013 after being diagnosed with lung cancer. Our sympathies are with the Lee family and friends.

FAMILIAR STRANGERS
A reflection by Declan Kiberd

Declan Kiberd, who is originally from Dublin, is currently Professor of Irish Studies at Notre Dame University.

(Opposite)
Natalie Ghazi from Nigeria taking a look at some turf. Not a lot of that in Nigeria!

Photograph: Denis Caroll

The signs said '*Irish Way*', or '*Waterford Drive*', but when I arrived in Notre Dame in mid-August the place didn't feel familiar at all. A hot Indiana light burned incessantly on fair skin, making me consider for the first time in my life the use of an umbrella for protection from the sun. And then, when it came, a hard, hard rain: not the soft Irish drizzle but a real downpour. My son, Rory, cavorted in that cooling water for a while, all whoops and giggles. The arrival of a twister sent him into ecstasies: "It's just like the movies". But even the rain began to pall in the end.

Rory fled into O'Rourke's bar, seeking consolation, but that took some time. He had just celebrated his 21st birthday and his passport said 'DOB 12.7.90'. The sharp-eyed security-man assumed that that meant his first alcoholic drink was still to come: 7 December 2011. He took some persuading that Irish passports give the day, month and year, in that order, and that Rory had been born on a day sacred to all Orangemen: 12 July 1990. By the time that was settled, Rory was already co-opted by the hard chaws: a real Irishman among 'the Irish'.

Despite this triumph, we wondered whether we would ever feel at home – but soon we did. After a few days on campus, we noticed how often we passed the same, now familar faces of people who, recognising us too, would say a warm 'hello'. There are indeed no strangers in Notre Dame: just friends who haven't yet met.

On the third evening, I noticed separate groups of male and female students wending their way to the start-of-academic-year Mass. It was a scene straight out of my own teenage years in Clontarf.

What came to impress me most about the Irish (no inverted, or perverted, commas now) at Notre Dame is the energy and enthusiasm with which they embrace their work, play and cultural identity. If only everyone back on the old island had a little more of that self-belief. I sometimes fear that Professors of Irish Studies will reach a point at which they feel that they are expounding a nation on the verge of disappearance. Yet the history of our people is filled with near-death experiences followed by glorious rallies and revivals. We always somehow rise again, a little like the Notre Dame footballers.

My Spring semester is spent back in my home place of Dublin, explaining Irish culture to visiting students from Notre Dame. At the start, they find it as baffling as I found South Bend: the craziness of Temple Bar on Friday nights, the narrow roads on which cars squeeze past each other at great speed, the tendency of buses to appear in twos or not at all. But eventually they also uncover a world not greatly different from the one they already know – in the rhythms of communal life; in the songs of their grandparents, now played on electric guitars in gastropubs; above all, in the hand of friendship extended to someone who just ten seconds ago was a stranger.

Can I have your autograph?

Photograph:
Malcolm McGettigan / BigOMedia

GATHERING-DOWN TO BUSINESS
Vivian Doyle-Kelly

I'm back in Dublin and walking into the Convention Centre on a freezing cold night. When I left Ireland in 1981 this area was decaying dockland. It was impossible then to have envisaged the splendid transformation it would undergo over the years.

Tonight I'm one of 700 people gathering from all over Ireland and the world with a shared connection – we trained and worked together in a major accountancy firm, and went on our separate ways, forging lives and careers elsewhere. We have returned for the KPMG alumni gathering dinner, with stories to share and experiences to swap.

Part of my tale begins decades earlier on a bright September day. The temperature was in the mid twenties and the sky was blue. Not a bad introduction to Montreal, my future home.

I remember I arrived mid-morning and registered a bustle expected from any major city. But with that bustle was a great ease, a sense that this was a nice place, a place where I would be happy to live. As I meet old friends and colleagues this evening, I'm glad to be able to tell them that my first impressions of Montreal were right. I quickly fell in love with the place, and within a few years started thinking of myself as a Canadian, almost without noticing it.

Sharing stories of entrepreneurship and the joys and heartache of setting up and running a business dominate a lot of the conversation. In Canada I set up my own energy-saving company, Eco-Watt. Tonight we reminisce about how, growing up in Ireland, we were always turning things off and closing the door for fear of a high ESB bill. I tell people that in Quebec we probably have some of the cheapest electricity costs and highest per-capita consumption in the world.

Down the years, while building the business, I have never lost touch with Ireland. It would be impossible to do so in Montreal anyway. The shamrock features on the City of Montreal flag and 40% of the francophone population of the Province of Quebec reputedly has Irish blood, primarily due to the wave of immigration during Famine times, when their integration into French Canada was facilitated by a common rural, Catholic background. Montreal's iconic St Patrick's Basilica was consecrated in 1847, demonstrating the existence of an established Irish community prior to the Famine.

I had known about *The Gathering* through work I do with Tourism Ireland in Montreal. All of those I meet at this special gathering agree that anything that helps keep the diaspora connected to Ireland is worthwhile.

For me, returning for our alumni gathering dinner was a great opportunity to catch up with people I started my career with but hadn't been in touch with in recent years. Like many present, my visits home had been more family-focused rather than a way of staying in contact with former colleagues.

We talk about how the Irish are so connected, and how it fascinates outsiders when we start a conversation with, "Where in Ireland are you from..?" The response is usually followed with, "Do you know so and so?" And of course the response is usually yes!

So on a chilly spring evening, it was fascinating to listen to people with whom I had worked closely at an early stage of my career, and to hear their stories and how their lives have progressed – a special gathering that I hope will be repeated soon.

Vivian Doyle-Kelly is a businessman and President of the Ireland-Canada Chamber of Commerce Montreal Chapter.

Evening falls on the transformed Dublin docklands.

Photograph: Mick Hunt

Some of those who attended the Stack Family gathering in Listowel, Co. Kerry. Photograph: Ann McNamee

Kinsella cousins. Photograph: AC Event Photography

The Rocha Family at the Sally Gap, Co. Wicklow in 1993.

CLUB ORANGE AND COMMUNION DRESSES

A reflection by Simone Rocha

Simone Rocha is a renowned Irish fashion designer and daughter of world-famous designer John Rocha.

To me, Ireland is home, and home is where the heart is. It is where I am from, and I am proud of that. My dad is from Hong Kong, but I was born in Mount Carmel Hospital in Dublin. Now, when I think of Mount Carmel, I think of the area where I had to take my driving test.

When I think of home, I think of Ranelagh, where I grew up: the old railway which is now the Luas, Jason's, which is now a Lidl store; long grass, green moss-covered walls, Moyne Road, Morton's, Windsor Road, shopping trolleys, and the foster-parent family across the road, Hatty and Mitsey.

When I think of 'hospice', I think of the people I know from home who have been hospice patients, including Pat, who made all my leathers and who shared a workplace with my parents in South William Street. I think about how he frequented Grogan's, and thinking of Grogan's, I am reminded of toasted cheese sandwiches with sachets of mayonnaise and mustard. And then I think of Glendalough – the smell, the fresh air, walking the bridges, and tying wishes on the wishing tree with Claireban Coffey.

I think of the National College of Art and Design in the Liberties: the chipper, communion dresses, the 123 bus, the Guinness Store House, the smell of hops and peat, and Thomas Street.

When I think of home, I think of Birr in Co. Offaly: pony camp, Grandad's bungalow, hay bales, boys, Club Orange, singing, sean-nós, *She Moves Through The Fair*, Grandad's funeral, Granny's funeral, Irish funerals, walking behind funerals, community halls, First Aid classes, choir.

I think of driving home from Belfast after a Seán Scully show, buying fireworks and driving up to the Wicklow Mountains to set them off. It is getting dark and we don't know where to stop. We go through the Sally Gap over the mountains to the sea, ending in Sandymount, setting off the fireworks into the night. I think of the sea, the sea, the sea – in Dublin and in Cork, at Roundstone and the Forty Foot.

Ireland is home and home is where the heart is, with family and friends and strangers; music, laughing, kissing at the canal, singing, cold water, Samuel Beckett, Francis Bacon, Louis Le Brocquy and Shane MacGowan.

Living and working in London, my studio walls are plastered with imagery from home: Perry Ogden's *Pony Kids*, my Granny's Mass cards, Eoin's lambs and Sally Gap. I am always influenced by home: the earth, the smell and the sea. It is built into me.

Glendalough.

Photograph: Joseph Carr

THE RHODE GATHERING
Claire O'Brien

Rhode is a tiny crossroads of a village in Co. Offaly. But everyone knows that Irish history is full of special gatherings at crossroads, and the Rhode Gathering was no exception.

It began on a rainy Friday evening, when passers-by were hauled from their cars to make up the 1,451 people who broke the world record for the *Rock the Boat* seated dance. Its symbolism set the tone for the weekend – a steady, cheerful trail of returning natives back on the road to Rhode.

The gathering was a chance for Michael Hynes to spend his first night in Rhode since he left more than 50 years ago. A sprightly industrial engineer, now living in upstate New York, he has travelled the world and stops by "very briefly" to see his family every couple of years – but this gathering was different. He'd never hung around much before, he said with a wry smile, because, "Most people forget me – it's been a long time!"

Even though he'd been in Ireland just three weeks earlier for his sister's 80th birthday, he couldn't miss the gathering and a chance to stay with his nephew in Rhode. "It was great, like a family reunion. My sister travelled from Galway, my nieces and nephews came from all over. We reminisced about things we had forgotten about. It was very enjoyable because we had such great memories of growing up here."

"I met a few people who haven't seen me in 50 years," he added, with a grin, "but it's not just the people who have changed in that time." The Rhode power station, which he remembers being built across the road from his home, is no longer on the landscape, but it's very much alive in the minds of the scores of men and their wives who returned for the ESB reunion to the town where their careers started in the 1960's.

Around every corner there was back-slapping and choruses of 'hail fellow, well met' as old acquaintances were renewed. For Peter Duffy, retired in Longford, it was a magical time and a special reunion. "They were wonderful people," he said, listing the names of dozens of men he had worked with and looked forward to seeing in the special Rhode museum and at the ESB reunion in O'Toole's pub.

Over sausages and sandwiches, and a cake in the shape of the power station's towers, they watched an ESB video of its history. The room came alive with the sound effects of the narrow-gauge railway, the grunts and rattles of wagons, the squealing of brakes, the hum of chat and the droning of machinery, all overlapping, as they must have done when the plant was in its heyday.

Some of the 1,451 people who broke the world record for the Rock the Boat seated dance in Rhode over the gathering weekend.

Photograph: Carol Ryan

Some of the 430 participants who took part in the School Olympics as part of the Rhode Gathering.

Photograph: Carol Ryan

But it was different for women, and Breda O'Leary, who has been living in Ealing Broadway in London for 48 years, had left Rhode on her 17th birthday to find work. "It's lovely to come back on a holiday," she said, in a still-strong Offaly accent. She had been delighted to get an invitation to the gathering. "We're all getting that bit older now. It's just nice to meet up with people and have a chat," she said pointing out Ann, whom she hadn't seen since they were in school together "many moons ago."

The iconic towers of the power station may be gone, but there's an electricity that powers Rhode still. "It's the power of community," said Niall Murphy from the Rhode Parish Gathering Committee. "And Rhode is a great, great community that we are so proud of."

Claire O'Brien is a freelance journalist and broadcaster based in the Midlands.

MANHATTAN DARKIE AT A COUNTRY GATHERING

A reflection by Patrick F. Wallace

Pat Wallace was the Director of the National Museum of Ireland for 23 years until his retirement in 2012.

(Opposite)
Jessica de Burca Montague pictured at the launch of the 'Gathering of the Vikings', part of the Clontarf Festival in association with Dublin City Council.

Photograph: Jason Clarke

It is the definite article which gives the ominous, almost biblical sense of foreboding to *The Gathering*. An Irish phrase like *Tar Abhaile* (Come Home!) might have softened if obscured somewhat what is undoubtedly a sincere invitation home to our diaspora. Be that as it may, the Irish are great at gatherings, particularly when they are spontaneous, as at funerals where there is no exclusion or selection and when anybody can turn up.

Gatherings take place every hour of every day and always will. Here, I would like to concentrate on a gathering captured in a photograph of 70 years ago. It locks forever the shared happiness of friends and neighbours at a country wedding in wartime Limerick. Being posed, of course it cannot convey the full reality and variety of life experience of the so-called Emergency with its LDF manoeuvres, flying boats, crackling radio messages both of the war and of a celebrated county hurling team. Nor does it convey anything of enforced food rationing or the difficulties of procuring cigarettes to which most of the two dozen or so people in the picture were addicted. The shared irritation of poor quality bicycle tubes and tyres was but another background experience which cannot be conveyed.

The central character at this gathering is a bespectacled, behatted elderly man, a family patriarch, a retired blacksmith who is seated outside his home with his family, friends and neighbours. He is at the right hand side of the bride (his eldest daughter), the groom and the maid of honour. The well turned out man between the bride and the dog was the

The unforeseen approach of change at a country gathering 70 years ago.

celebrated Gaelic Games correspondent of the local newspaper and husband of the maid of honour. The bride was marrying relatively late. She was for long a buttermaker at the local creamery which is where she had met her husband, a fitter who had come to install new machinery. Her youngest sister, a buttermaker at another creamery stands behind her alongside her intended, a builder and handyman.

Their other sister who was the life and soul of their home since their mother died, had returned home from nursing in London to care for the patriarchal father. She sits at the right end of the seated group to the left of her own fiancé, a machine driver from the West, who later became a celebrated tractor salesman. While he may not have shared the patriarch's politics, they shared a love of greyhounds which they both bred. It is therefore appropriate and in ways symbolic that he holds a beloved dog called 'Manhattan Darkie'.

The three sons of the family stand in the back row, one with outstretched arms on the shoulders of a neighbour, a horse breeder. This son worked for years as a barman in the city before having to emigrate to the steelworks of Lincolnshire where he died in the early 1970's. The youngest son, then an architect in Dublin stands to the right of the bespectacled best man, a brother of the groom. The oldest son (second from the right) followed his father as a blacksmith. There is no sense among the members of this optimistic gathering that a tidal wave of mechanisation would destroy most of the forges in the country within 20 years. Maybe the apprentice on the left front row who was later to introduce electric welding in his own establishment, in his own way, is the harbinger of an industrialised future.

176

Returning to the photograph, the personable young woman at the front was a farmer's daughter, a family friend. She later married a sign painter and county hurler and remained close to the middle daughter of the family until her own untimely death. Her sister, who never married, looks over the shoulder of the best man in the back row. The groom's niece, later a distinguished sister in religion, sits between the bride and groom.

There is a quiet rural dignity among the people at this gathering. What comes across is the strength and assurance of a small community with deep roots, where everyone knows everyone, where they had come from and what they were capable of. Such a community would be difficult to come upon today so much has our world changed in seven decades.

The old man would have witnessed the split in nationalism with Parnell, would have seen the lead up to Independence, the RIC, the Tans, the Civil War, the Economic War and the Blueshirts. He would have also witnessed the birth and the coming of age of the motor car. For the bride's generation "there was nothing to be got from grumbling" as their mantra had it. Later, they would endure the awful 1950's relieved only by the benefits of rural electrification. They would rejoice in the educational opportunities enjoyed by their children in the 1960's and afterwards. Few of them survived to see the self-inflicted collapse of organised Catholicism, which removed a perceived threat to Ulster Protestants who then were able to find the confidence to conclude the historic Good Friday Agreement.

They would have been delighted with the resulting state of Anglo-Irish relations which are at their best in several centuries. They wouldn't have believed that Queen Elizabeth would come to Ireland and speak in Irish to our President at Dublin Castle. Mind you, they would be appalled that gambling banks, a lack of concern for communal good, and a wanton absence of official regulation would have allowed a native government and its senior civil service to recklessly squander our economic good health. However, their experiences over many decades would have taught them that bad times don't last forever and that every wheel comes full circle.

Would I have liked to have been present at the gathering in the photograph? Well, in a way I was. The patriarch was my grandfather. He lived on for another five years during which he lost his sight one morning as he was reading a report of a hurling match. He died 12 days before I was born.

ABBEY FISHERMEN GATHERING
Sharon Slater

For centuries, the Abbey Fishermen were an integral part of Limerick city life. The Clancy, Hayes, McNamara, Liddy, Shanny, Hartigan, O'Connor and O'Dwyer families lived in areas such as the King's Island, the Parish, and the Park, earning their living fishing salmon, eel and peal in the Shannon and Abbey Rivers.

These hard-working people practiced a unique snap fishing craft based on ancient Brehon laws, successions and traditions passed down through generations. Hundreds of people were supported by this activity, right up to the advent of the Ardnacrusha Hydroelectric Scheme in the 1930's. By this time only four families – the Clancys, Hayes, McNamaras and Shannys – still actively fished the river.

The Abbey Fishermen Gathering brought members of these four families together again to remember, to reconnect, and to celebrate the contribution they had made to Limerick life. A call-out was issued to descendants abroad to come back to Limerick to meet their family members, old neighbours and friends, to share memories and stories of their ancestors.

The nostalgic weekend started with a gathering of all the visitors in the heart of Abbey Fishermen territory, the King's Island Community Centre. It was an emotional evening, as connections were made and stories were swapped with descendants from the US and England. Family members who had never met before, or who had not seen each other in some cases in over 50 years, were reunited. With the Hayes family, for

(Opposite above)
On the river like their descendants are from left: John Shanny, Charlie Clancy, Ger Hayes and Anthony McNamara.

(Opposite below)
Anthony McNamara and Ger Hayes hoping to land a catch.

Photographs: Seán Curtin

example, three brothers and a sister who were spread across the world came together in the home of their parents.

A walking tour of the old Abbey area where most of the Abbey Fishermen and their families lived took the group to O'Dwyer's Bridge and then to St. Mary's Church where they saw a special mural depicting the Abbey Fishermen. Along the way there were stops at St Mary's Band Hall and St Mary's Cathedral to look at the Shanny, Clancy and Hayes graves. The Shanny grave was particularly poignant for the Shanny family members, as they had not known it was there.

There was a photographic exhibition with pictures of grandfathers that their descendants had never seen and a talk with a slide show featuring images and photographs of members of the Abbey Fishermen families emigrating due to the loss of their livelihood. In the audience was 92-year-old Joe Elligot, who vividly remembered fishing with the Abbey Fisherman, and the 'Battle of the Tail Race' in July 1932. This was a protest, which resulted in a confrontation with the army, police and water bailiffs, by the fishermen at the fact that the fishing grounds were to be sacrificed to the new hydroelectric scheme.

Boat trips on the Abbey and Shannon rivers up to Ardnacrusha involved many tears for those who had never experienced what it was like every day on the water for their fathers and grandfathers. There were magical memories exchanged, fuelled by talks and stories on the history of the Abbey Fishermen. Most of all, friends and relations reconnected, or connected for the first time, and the ties between the Clancy, Hayes, McNamara and Shanny families were strengthened – bonds that no doubt will endure.

Sharon Slater is a historical and genealogical researcher based in Co. Limerick.

(Above)
The Abbey Fishermen in action.
(Left)
Three members of the Abbey Fishermen families pictured in the Navy.

This lady seemed to enjoy the Shantalla 70th birthday celebration despite the weather.

Photograph: Andrew Downes

WHEN THE GIFT IS THE MOMENT

A reflection by Orla Tinsley

Orla Tinsley is a campaigner and journalist from Kildare.

In the summer of 2012, I stood inside the new Cystic Fibrosis (CF) Unit at St Vincent's University Hospital in Dublin with a friend. Exactly eight years earlier my part in the campaign to build the unit began. It was eight years of promises made and promises broken, paths changed and so many lives lost. For me it was over 50 hospitalisations, three lung collapses and who knows how many hours of life away from family and friends.

Our triumph at getting the unit built was that of 'people power' and hard work; of positive thinking, love and sacrifice. Standing there in that moment, the years swept through me faster than I could register, as though a limb I didn't realise had left me back then had re-attached.

The summer of 2005 when the campaign began was one of the hottest on record. The Celtic Tiger was raging and while my friends were busy checking out colleges, I was busy deciding to which adult hospital I would transfer the care of my cystic fibrosis. St Vincent's University Hospital in Dublin was the designated national referral centre, and despite not having international standards of care, with single isolation rooms for treatment, I figured that when change happened, it would happen there first.

I spent most days that summer, in between the intravenous treatment and physiotherapy, lounging on the grass behind the wards with my friend, Martha, who made life on the inside as a 'CFer' easier. We both hated the term 'CFer', with its suggestion that we were some sort of unique species. We were human. We hated the labels, we hated the damn place and we hated the limitations. Martha, at 23, travelled whenever she wasn't 'on the inside' – which had elevated to every few weeks by the time I met her. She sought out new adventures in any country to which the cheapest flights would take her.

We shared a room on and off for two months, along with four seriously unwell, elderly ladies who rotated in and out. We moved between helping them and – when it got to be too much – running away from them. This was youth then, dragging the IV stand out to the chair in the hall at 4am to snooze sitting up, because the noises in the room were like physical inflictions of sadness. We were a different kind of Irish youth, our disco a music that had never been heard before, blasting all night with no release.

Most of my post-Leaving Cert friends were off in sunny somewhere-or-other, planning their college years and certain of the future. I burned to be a writer, and so, I wrote all the time. It was all I could do.

There's a quotation from Mark Twain that my friend Martha stuck on the fridge of her tiny apartment in Pembroke Road: *Twenty years from now you will be more disappointed by the things you didn't do than by the ones you did. So throw off the bowlines. Sail away from the safe harbor. Catch the trade winds in your sails. Explore. Dream. Discover.*

Martha died from complications of Cystic Fibrosis, in the same bed I had left just a few days earlier. Afterwards, I wrote Mark Twain's words down and imprinted them into my gut.

Illness makes you see things differently. Alcohol seems stupid, smoking moronic, and people who waste time are people who waste you. Melodrama, a hallmark of so many teenage conversations, hurts the mind and wounds the heart.

The urgency to *do it now* is all-encompassing, and so, youth becomes this strange amalgamation of enthusiastic panic and a substantial nod to the responsible, respecting your illness but also rebelling from its restraints. And then death happens to someone you love. It teaches you compassion, not to be angry at the colleges that rejected you or the slots of supposed youthful rites of passage that you couldn't fit into.

When I stood in the new Cystic Fibrosis Unit in the summer of 2012, it had been exactly eight years since I had written my first piece for *The Irish Times*. I had kept writing at every chance. Every time a promise was broken, every time someone died, every time a government official delayed the situation. There is a drive that comes from constant illness, and an even greater one that comes from death, like an endless supply of a drug that keeps you reeling like a wound-up doll that you cannot stop.

Most of my friends have emigrated now. Some went off on great adventures; some left filled with anger and resentment about the economic situation, wishing someone would flip a switch and make times good again.

Reflecting, in this the year of *The Gathering*, I am glad to say that for people with CF in Ireland, life has happened in reverse. We have a greater ability to stay alive. Facilities are slowly improving countrywide, and new treatments mean that for the first time since the CF gene was discovered in 1989, we now have the closest thing to a cure for some people.

But cure or no cure, the gift is the moment and remembering to carpe diem. It's not about money or achievement, although those things are nice; it's the steps we take to move towards life, each moment enriched by loving what we have and the people we are with.

'Paper Dolls' in Merrion Square Park, Dublin, as part of the St. Patrick's weekend celebrations.

Photograph: Suzanne Cummins

(Above)
Antonio Santiago from Dallas, Texas receives some Banjo tuition from Eugene Quinn from The Irish House Party band at the 'Killoe in the Capital' gathering event.   Photographer: Paul Devaney

(Below)
What a quacking day it was at the Duck-a-Thon, Tralee!
Photograph: Dylan Harnett

(Opposite above)
Farleys 50th, Kinsale, Co.Cork.   Photograph: Uwe Ditz

(Opposite below)
Percy's Party, Mohill, Co. Leitrim.   Photograph: Therese Foy

101-year-old Jackie 'The Farmer' O'Sullivan from Ballagh, Killarney, was the first to register for the Guinness Book of Records Largest Same Name Gathering attempt at the O'Sullivan Clan Gathering in Sneem, Co. Kerry.

Photograph:
Valerie O'Sullivan

A GATHERING PLAY
A reflection by Michael Harding

Michael Harding is an Irish novelist and playwright and Irish Times columnist.

(The following speech is from a work-in-progress: a stage play which tracks the life of an Irish emigrant in Canada.)

"There once was a man who left Westmeath 60 years ago and headed for America. He landed in Chicago, but went across the border and made his way to Saskatoon in Canada, where he had relations, but when he got there they were just moving off. Going out the door. They left him there on his own and he was very lonesome, so he decided to go home the next day. But the next day he met another Irishman who said there was a party in his house that night so he stayed for the *craic*. And when the party started, someone said the Irish keep pigs in their houses. He didn't like that so they started arguing and then shouting and eventually he said, "I'll tell you something for nothing, you Canadian jack ass; a dog looks up at ye, a cat looks down at ye, but only a pig looks you in the eye. Do you get me?"

The Canadian didn't get him. So he said, "You're looking me in the eye, my good man, and I know what I'm looking at."

But the Canadian said, "I dont know what you're talking about." So the Irishman hit him in the face.

"Do you know what I'm getting at now?" he inquired.

189

And then the place exploded and they thrashed the shop and so the Irishman had to vanish. So he went to the outskirts of the town and found a job in a bar for a few weeks. And a man came into the bar one day and said he had a truck and a few guys were driving north to Yellow Knife for work, and if he paid for his part of the gas he could go with them.

So off he went in the truck, and they landed in a place far north of Yellow Knife, and the place was mostly populated by First Nation People.

"Mother of Jesus," said the Irishman, "nothing but Indians. And little huts. And smoke. And wolves in the woods."

But in the end they landed in a place where the men were working for an oil company, and they went into a cabin where 12 big oilmen were sitting around a table, and a big moose on the middle of the table, 12 hundredweight, and they were eating it with their hands.

The fellow who drove the truck kicked snow off his boots and said to the Irishman, "Come over to the window."

They looked out and he pointed to where the oil rigs were. "Did you ever work on one of them?"

"No," said the Irishman, "I never did."

"There's money to be made on the oil rigs," his companion said.

So he started that afternoon at 4pm.

"But I got nothing to eat yet," he said, so the bossman said, "Go into the canteen and tell the chef you're working for Axel-Joe."

So he went in and the chef put up a big roast of beef to him and he ate some, and he was feeling his pockets to see what money was left when the little woman who was serving came over and she said, "Do you want more?" And he said, "Well, be God I will," and afterwards he got up and said, "How much is that?" And the little woman said, "Oh no, you're working for Axel-Joe."

Well, he would have eaten the entire beef if he had known that. But the little woman was smiling at him, and after a few months she was still feeding him and he had money rat-holed away in the snow, and he learned that she was a First Nation person or what he used to call an Eskimo, but that didn't bother him because he was already in love with her.

"Will you come home to Ireland with me?," he said to her one day. But she refused. She was prepared to go as far as Newfoundland, 'cos she had cousins there. But he said, "I couldn't go to Newfoundland. I want to go home to Mullingar."

But the way she smiled at him meant that he couldn't resist, so eventually he went to Newfoundland with her and they stayed there 38 years, and every year when he sat down at his Christmas dinner he would make a joke that he was half way home to Mullingar.

Eventually she was killed in a car accident out near St Brides and he was broken hearted.

A moose landed on the windscreen, and when the firemen came to take her out of the wreckage, her body and the body of the moose were all tangled together beneath the car and the snow had turned red.

After that he got a home help to make his dinner each day, and when a postcard arrived one morning from Ireland inviting him to *The Gathering* he was moved to tears, and then the postcard went missing and he accused the home help of throwing it out with the rubbish, which was not true. Eventually she found it under his pillow. But it didn't matter because he was too old by then to ever see Ireland again."

GLAOCH – THE PRESIDENT'S CALL
Nuala O'Connor

At the invitation of President Michael D. Higgins, Irish artists, musicians, poets and playwrights gathered at Áras an Uachtaráin for a magical three days in February to celebrate and showcase Ireland's rich creativity to the world.

'Glaoch – The President's Call' was a unique coming together of talented Irish people, filmed for a special one-hour RTE documentary. In a first in Irish broadcasting history, it was also live-streamed worldwide on the RTE Player and YouTube channel on St Patrick's Day, receiving over a million hits from the diaspora around the globe.

Dedicated to Irish people everywhere, this special programme was a call from President Higgins to Irish people "to engage with the valuable resource that is our culture, to look to our creative possibilities and to project our Irishness into the world in the positive way that has been the achievement of our artists and cultural workers."

Áras an Uachtaráin, the 18th century home of Irish presidents, is set amongst one of the great urban parklands in Europe, and rarely has it been shown in such intimate detail as it was over these unforgettable three days. Beautifully presented and lit for the occasion, the four state rooms, the entrance hall and the President's study were transformed into performance spaces and inhabited by a succession of Irish artists of every discipline, generation and background.

President Higgins is a poet, a theatre goer, an avid reader, an Irish speaker and a music fan, with tastes ranging from traditional to contemporary. He is described in the film

President Higgins and singer Christy Moore in Áras an Uachtaráin at the filming of Glaoch - The President's Call.

Photograph: Richard Gilligan

193

by Bono as a 'kindred spirit' for the artistic community in Ireland, and along with his wife, Sabina, was a fitting host for this great gathering.

Many performances and interviews for the documentary addressed the ways in which attachment to place and emigration charged the engine of Irish creativity in the arts over many generations.

Playwright Tom Murphy's partnership with Druid Theatre Company was represented in Glaoch in a reading from his play *Famine* by actress, Marie Mullen, and in a conversation between Murphy, President Higgins and Druid Director, Garry Hynes.

More recent accounts of the Irish emigration experience in Britain were presented by singer Imelda May in her tender song about life on the dole in London, *Kentish Town*, and in writer Joseph O'Connor's poignant reading, *Airspace*, reflecting on the richness and diversity of the Irish experience and perspective.

Singer Christy Moore chatted with the President about home and the centrality of the local and parochial in the Irish imagination. He told of visiting a west Cork farm with the singer/songwriter, John Spillane. This 'green jewel' was where Spillane's mother was born and where each field had a name, a function and an identity as defined as any other

Bono and President Higgins.

Photograph: Richard Gilligan

Imelda May and her husband Darrel Higham.

Photograph: Johnny Savage

living thing. This place was the inspiration for John's song, *Gortatagort*, half lament, half praise song, which was performed by Christy and is embedded in his repertoire.

Poet Séamus Heaney spoke of Ireland as a country "which respects poets". Singer Iarla Ó Lionáird, accompanied by guitarist Steve Cooney, performed a version of the old Irish song, *Siuil a Rún*, translated by the first President of Ireland, Douglas Hyde.

Paula Meehan gave an arresting reading of her poem, *Home*, while poet, Louis de Paor, read *An Glaoch*, a bilingual poem he created for this project. Young Roisín O' gave a virtuoso singing performance, and rock band, The Script, performed *Hall of Fame* jubilantly endorsing Irish talent and creative energy. There was music from Glen Hansard and Lisa Hannigan, while the final set of tunes came from Martin Hayes, Peadar O'Riada and David Power.

It was as if, in the President's closing words, "the culture, the wide space of the culture has the possibility to transform everything."

Nuala O'Connor, formally a radio producer with RTE, is an independent documentary film-maker and co-founder of Hummingbird Productions and SouthWind Blows.

A HOME BIRD AT HEART
A reflection by Katie Taylor

Katie Taylor is one of the world's top female amateur boxers and a winner of a gold medal at the Olympic Games in London.

(Opposite)
Katie Taylor, celebrates after being declared the winner over Sofya Ochigava of Russia, in their women's light 60kg final at the London 2012 Olympics.

Photograph: Ray McManus / Sportsfile

I have always been proud to be Irish and I love my country. I wear the Irish vest with great pride, and to hear the national anthem being sung before a big fight really lifts my heart.

I know Ireland has been through tough times economically, but our sense of humour, positive attitude and strong character will get us through. It has done so in the past, and I firmly believe will continue to do so in the future.

There are many families who are having it hard. I can see it around me where I live on a council estate in Co. Wicklow. A lot of my neighbours are affected by the recession – good, decent, working-class people.

It is very sad that families have to say goodbye to their loved ones who have to emigrate to find work. I see lots of young Irish people when I am travelling who have left Ireland to start a new life. My own brother is in that situation. He has a wife and young child and is applying for a job in the US because he can't get work here. I am hoping and praying that he doesn't have to go. It would break my heart, and my parents' hearts, if he left.

The Gathering has been a great initiative and has had a positive impact on the country. People are talking about it at home and abroad. It reminds people of their Irishness and is helping to keep Irish people connected at home.

Everyone loves the Irish, and everywhere I go to fight around the world there is phenomenal support and Irish people there to cheer me on. They keep me going. But I am a 'home bird' at heart and there is no place like Ireland, the mountains and the scenery, and the people. I had an opportunity to go professional and move to the US but it was more important to me to be able to continue to fight as an amateur in the green vest, and to live in Ireland, no matter what the financial attractions. There is no price on being able to box for your country.

The Olympics and winning gold for Ireland have been the highlight of my career. I love hearing people tell me where they watched my fight when I won gold. I am thrilled that I am able to lift people's spirits through my sport.

I have always followed my dreams, so my message to people is to follow your dreams too. I am lucky in that I have a great family and friends, and am part of a great country.

I would say to people that when things are tough, try to be positive. You will get through it. When I am going through tough times I turn to God. I lean on him because there is nothing he won't do for you. Proverbs, Chapter 3, sums this up: "*Trust in the Lord with all your heart and lean not on your own understanding; in all your ways acknowledge him, and he will make your paths straight.*"

Katie in action.

Photograph: Cathal Noonan / INPHO

GATHERING OF IRISH WOLFHOUNDS
Eddie Gilsenan

Farmleigh House in the Phoenix Park basked in glorious sunshine for a somewhat unusual gathering of 65 Irish Wolfhounds who came with their owners from far and wide including France, Spain, Slovakia and the UK.

Irish Wolfhounds have a proud tradition in Irish history dating back hundreds of years, surviving near-extinction, famine and war. They are also one of the five symbols of Ireland, along with the harp, the shamrock, the round tower and the sunburst.

The Irish Wolfhound, or Cú, was used by the ancient Irish for fighting and hunting. It was a sight hound for the ancient chiefs and kings of Ireland and considered to be a royal dog and not for general ownership. Many were exported to other countries as gifts or as tributes from the Irish people.

A colour party of retired Irish soldiers, led by a lone piper and the Irish Wolfhound mascot, Keelagh, started the event which centred on the Irish Wolfhound Championship Show.

There was adjudication in different classes, from puppy to veteran. They included tallest wolfhound, best head, brace and the children's class, where everyone was a winner.

Over 10,000 people passed through the Phoenix Park on the day and many were lucky enough to catch a glimpse of these gentle giants.

Eddie Gilsenan is a member of the Irish Wolfhound Club of Ireland.

Photographs:
Patrick Hugh Lynch

*Lisa Sarsfield of the Buí Bolg
Theatre Group helps launch
the New Year's Eve Festival,
which officially marked the
start of The Gathering.*

*Photograph: Bryan O'Brien /
The Irish Times*

WHY CAN'T I?

A reflection by John Geoghegan

John Geoghegan is Director of the World Scout Federation.

(Opposite above)
Visitors at the Bloom festival in the Phoenix Park.

Photograph: Cyril Byrne / The Irish Times

(Opposite below)
The St Colmcille Pageant which was part of the Cos Cos Festival in Drumcliffe, Rathcormac, Co. Sligo.

Photograph: Conor Doherty

A fish only really understands what water is when he is out of it.

In 1987, I arrived in London from Ireland to work for the British Red Cross as National Youth Officer, and although we spoke the same language, looked at the same TV, and listened to the same music, I discovered that I was different – very different – to all my colleagues!

I quickly understood that being 'different' is an asset. It gives you cover to speak up, to question the status quo, and to help bring about real change and succeed where others may fail.

Within three years I had joined the International Red Cross, where I experienced many international crises first hand. I was the first foreign youth worker into China after the Tiananmen Square protests. I was part of a team that challenged Serbs and Croats to work with Muslims in Bosnia in those terrible times of conflict and post-conflict – dedicated professionals who literally put their lives on the line to save the most vulnerable people in post-Soviet Europe and Eurasia. I spent three years in Vietnam, where 20,000 houses and 200 schools were built by the Red Cross, and hundreds of thousands fed and clothed. We helped bring the Vietnamese and Americans together to aid the victims of Agent Orange.

In each of the 93 countries I have visited for work, I have always been welcomed with open arms. Over the years, I have been lucky enough to have worked with an amazing range of people – kings, presidents, ministers, princes, princesses and business leaders, but also with brave and inspiring volunteers, the most dignified and admirable people for whom money is never part of their lives.

My daily life brings me in contact with a variety of nationalities. But I am still that Raheny guy who boarded the ferry in Dun Laoghaire with a terrible hangover after his 'American Wake' over a quarter of a century ago. In my role as Director of the World Scouting Foundation, I sit in a small office in Geneva, working a network of global leaders – all for the benefit of helping young people throughout the world. Together, we have inspired over 12 million hours of community service in the past six months alone.

I've been lucky enough to achieve a lot, possibly because my motto is: Why can't I? And it's my motto because I'm Irish, learned through osmosis from the day I was born.

My father's mother was from a Collins family in Kerry; his father an RIC constable stationed in the town. Despite their differences, they married, and my dad arrived. My mother's parents were deeply involved in the GPO in 1916, and despite my dad's RIC family background, they still got together. These seemingly impossible barriers were no barriers to them.

In my mid-teens I made contact with two amazing men, Paul Browne and Mike Loder, working on either side of the religious divide in Belfast, bringing Scouts from each community together with Scouts from the South at a time when few even crossed the border.

'Impossible' is not a word that any of these people used!

While I have degrees in leadership and management they are only affirmation of what I learned in one of the best management schools in the world – Scouting Ireland. This amazing organization, with its generations of inspired and inspiring volunteers, left an impact: a shy teenager transformed into a confident global operator, thanks to the faith of the men and women involved in it. It is what they do best.

A fish doesn't realise what water is until he's out of it. My Crumlin-born wife Eimear and I are very proud of our three teenage kids, who have all grown up away from Ireland. They stand tall, can look anyone in the eye, and feel confident. They face the challenges of life with a sense of humour and adventure – and maybe most important, because they're Irish, they seem to believe that nothing is impossible! Our kids, who have been out of Irish water but still consider themselves Irish, and Eimear and I, we all value our roots. For us, Irishness works.

The tapestry created by the 5th class students at Scoil Naomh Maodhóg, showing family crests of the pupils in the school.

Photograph:
Catherine MacPartlin

FERNS GATHERING
A Primary School's Perspective
Colm Ó Tiarnaigh

As the principal of Scoil Naomh Maodhóg in Ferns, Co. Wexford, it was with tentative interest and a little trepidation that I attended a public meeting in Ferns Community Centre in September 2012. We heard of initial plans for a weekend designed to celebrate the medieval heritage of our village as part of *The Gathering* project. In my wildest imagination I could not have envisaged the breadth and scope of what was to come in terms of community co-operation, celebration of national and local heritage and a learning experience for the children of our school.

At the meeting, I suggested a Christmas card be created by pupils in the local primary schools to serve as an invitation to people to come and visit. The cards were sent to over 14 countries, from as close as England and as far away as New Zealand.

Some families really got into the spirit of the project. James Lawlor and his little sister, Niamh, are a good example. They sent a card to their aunt and uncle in Florida and plans were put in place for them to come home for the gathering weekend.

And what a weekend it was. the launch parade was quite the spectacle on Friday night with the whole village turning out dressed in medieval clothes and marching from St Mary's Abbey up to Ferns Castle. The castle grounds were turned into a medieval village with lots of different activities and demonstrations and a medieval style banquet on Saturday night. It was a wonderful celebration, with locally sourced food and music adding to the occasion.

We are lucky to have the ruins of the MacMurrough Kavanagh Norman Castle as the backdrop to our school but it took the Ferns gathering weekend to reinvigorate the pupils' sense of their historic heritage.

Colm Ó Tiarnaigh is the principal of Scoil Naomh Maodhóg in Ferns.

(Top left)
A map showing where Gathering invite cards were sent all over the world.

(Top right)
James Lawlor is pictured posting his Christmas Card Gathering invite to his Aunt Sharon in Florida, with pupils from Scoil Naomh Maodhóg.

(Below)
Children from Scoil Naomh Maodhóg, Ferns attacking St. Mary's Augustinian Abbey where Dermot MacMurrough was in hiding, during a Ferns Gathering Festival event.

Photographs:
Colm Ó Tiarnaigh

Granny meets the next generation at the Mount Dalton gathering, Rathconrath, Co. Westmeath

Photograph: Michael Farrugia

Jean Winston (left) and Eileen McGarvey, pictured at the Pantomime Reunion at Ramelton Town Hall in Co. Donegal

Photograph: Bryan O'Brien / The Irish Times

*Micheál pictured at the 2010 All Ireland
Senior Football Final, Cork Vs Down, at Croke
Park. The game marked his last All Ireland
Final to commentate on.*

Photograph: Cathal Noonan/INPHO

THE GATHERING
A reflection by Micheál Ó Muircheartaigh

Micheál Ó Muircheartaigh is a retired GAA commentator.

The word 'gathering' springs to my mind quite often, perhaps because it can be regarded as a part of what we are as a race of humankind. As early as childhood the local gatherings on Fair Days, Pattern Days and other seasonal events struck a chord.

Before long, tales of gatherings further afield invaded the same mind as I watched people prepare to travel to some faraway places in anticipation of some wonder out of the ordinary.

Killorglin's Puck Fair – whose origins are almost lost in antiquity – is a good example for Kerry folk. The Fair, in which animals of all kinds are offered for sale, is distinguished by the fact that it has its very own Gathering Day on August 10th, just prior to the action day. It gained further lustre while still in its infancy when a third day, known as Scattering Day, became a welcome appendage.

I have memories also of witnessing the ritual of people preparing to set off for an All-Ireland Final in Croke Park, or 'Jones's Road', as that particular gathering place was referred to by some people. To my young mind, those followers of sport were going on an adventure. The initial part of the journey from Dingle to Tralee would be on the narrow gauge railway, and then on the ghost train through the night to Croke Park, immortalised in verse by the wordsmith Sigerson Clifford.

Ever since I am of the opinion that all gatherings entail a smidgeon of adventure, and indeed the Gaelic Athletic Association has supplied an endless stream of such events for well over 100 years. For west Kerry people, the narrow gauge may have succumbed to progress but the 'Ghost' lives on as a state of mind for current travellers, for whom 'travelling' to a match remains an integral part of any worthwhile gathering.

Did not the late Con Houlihan, who was living in Dublin at the time, once journey to his home in Kerry on the eve of an All-Ireland Final in order to fully imbibe the magic of a final by really travelling to it on the morrow, rather than merely strolling across the Liffey to Croke Park, his particular Mecca!

The first GAA gathering took place on the 1st November 1884. Only six people accepted an invitation from Michael Cusack to attend a meeting in Hayes Hotel, Thurles, for the purpose of founding an organisation to cater for native Irish sports. It was a disparate group that included two athletes, two journalists, an international rugby player and member of the Royal Irish Constabulary. From their deliberations and decisions a movement developed that has become a vital element in the psyche of Irish life.

It spread to every parish in the country, and by degrees has grown to be a cornerstone in the sporting and social scenes of the respective communities. As a consequence, myriads of 'gatherings' have materialised, the memory of which endures. Indeed, in this year of *The Gathering* at national level, the lure that twinkles in the same memory has brought many emigrants back on a special visit to re-kindle the joys of the past and to revel in the joys of the present.

Those same emigrants have fostered an element of that part of Irish life in their new surroundings in all quarters of the world. There are now over 400 GAA clubs outside of Ireland, and the name of each and every one stands proudly, side by side with the home ones, on the walls to the right and left of the entrance to Croke Park's Museum.

Those external units would not have comparable facilities with those of the home clubs and that is understandable, but there is no doubting the fact that the souls are equal and entirely compatible. I have had the privilege of seeing many of GAA clubs in places as far apart as North and South America, Australia, Europe, Asia and India, and of course our neighbouring lands of Wales, England, Scotland and the Isle of Man.

They value their seasonal gatherings and in some cases travel thousands of miles to compete at regional championships or events. Medals and other awards gleaned by the lucky few are treasured as much as All-Ireland medals back at home base.
Aside from playing the games, it is good to see how those Irish units abroad extend a hearty welcome to people of other nationalities who wish to be part of the show, and from my observation that spirit enhances the gatherings.

How often has it been stated that 'sport is great'? And when all is said and done, the joys of participation and comradeship are its greatest legacies. They lie close to the heart of the soul of real sport. Here's to the next gathering we attend, and there is nothing wrong with the outlook that it could well be the best ever.

Maybe someday a gathering of representatives from all GAA clubs the world over can be arranged for Croke Park, Dublin, Ireland. What a spirit would pour forth from it!

Clash of the Ash.

Photograph: James Crombie / INPHO

THE CARBERY GATHERING
Carlow

It was a special day for 181 direct descendants of Paul and Kathleen Carbery as they gathered at the Carlow Rugby Club.

Paul and Kathleen were married in 1936 and had 13 children. 12 of the siblings were there on the day except for Brendan. The young priest died in a tragic car accident in 1973 at the age of 28.

The 12 siblings lined up in order of age. From left are Pauline, Madeline, Dan, Michael, Des, Maurice, Kay, Frances, Mary, Brian, Eugene and Clare.

Photograph: Marcus Carbery

Family members came from Kansas, Colorado, Canada, France and the UK for the celebration which was organised by cousin, Paula Hughes. Three generations indulged in many activities including the expected sing song and a slideshow chronicling the family line from Paul and Kathleen's honeymoon in Switzerland in 1936 to the present day.

THE CARRIG-HILL GATHERING
Carlow

The Carrig and Hill gathering was very special, centred around the christening of Roric Carrig who was brought home to Ireland by his parents from Toronto, Canada.

His dad Ronan left Ireland three years ago. He and his wife Jennifer were joined by three generations of the Carrig clan and Jennifer's parents at the Talbot Hotel in Carlow.

Roric met his cousins, Daniel and Luisne, aged four and 18 months for the first time and after the ceremony it was on to the Carrig family home where there was home-made chocolate biscuit cake and a drop or two of Canadian whiskey - which many declared wasn't a patch on the Irish stuff!

Proud parents Ronan and Jennifer Carrig, with grandmother/ godmother Kathleen Carrig, watch as Father Cummins baptises baby Roric during a special gathering.

Photograph: Karen Carrig

GROWING UP AS AN ARTIST
IN IRELAND

A reflection by Pauline Bewick

Pauline Bewick is one of Ireland's best known contemporary artists.

The Bewick family originally descended from Norway. The Vikings sailed over from Bervick to Northumbria in Northern England. The 18th century wood engraver and naturalist, Thomas Bewick, was my great-great-great-granduncle. However, it was my mother Alice ('Harry') Graham-Bewick who was the formative influence in my life. She was half Newcastle, half Scottish.

In 1938 she ran away to Ireland from her alcoholic husband, Corbett Bewick, bringing me, aged two-and-a-half, and my sister, aged seven, to Kenmare in Co. Kerry, where she fostered two orphaned children, Lucy and Michael. She was like a hippie. She didn't pretend, and she didn't offend. She had no religion, was a vegetarian and wore long bright coloured stockings and a green coat. (I recall that the old women of Ireland then wore black shawls.) She always encouraged us children to paint and draw. I did my first pencil sketches at two-and-a-half years of age, which my mother always kept. I continued to paint and draw obsessively all my life.

After nine years we moved to Northern Ireland, where we lived in a caravan, and then on to England and Wales. We lived on a boat on the Kennet and Avon canal and I continued to paint copiously instead of doing school work, which was difficult due to my dyslexia. Then Alice – now 'Harry' – got a job as a vegetarian cook in two progressive schools, and she enrolled me as a pupil. My sister Hazel returned to Newcastle to her grandparents.

(Opposite)
Woman and Loddon Lilies 1987
Pauline Bewick.

We came back to Ireland in 1949, bringing with us our 35-foot boat to live in Passage West in Cork. One day the boat sprang a leak and my mother and I packed our bags and

217

went to Dublin, where she enrolled me in the National College of Art and Design. It was in the early 1950's and I was accepted for my portfolio drawings. One of the art teachers used to mutter crossly about, "these young girls going about with their bottoms encased in trousers". Another man, who looked after the 'Living Art' Exhibitions, used to get terribly annoyed with me and thought my pictures were far too explicit. He spotted that I didn't wear a bra. The men disapproved, yet they noticed. That was the atmosphere of the 1950's.

In 1963 I married the psychiatrist, Pat Melia, and had two daughters, Poppy and Holly, who also became artists. I yearned for a country upbringing for the girls, so we moved back to Kerry in 1973 and built a home in a beautiful remote valley. My style of freedom has drawn some critics over the years, but now things are so different and people relish the sensuality. I have become, however, rather prudish myself. A section of the media has gone over the top in recent times and is positively kinky. I am totally natural and for nature, but I think the media has gone unnaturally far.

I have found that Irish people appreciate and love art, they being of a creative nature, with open, rich minds, and that includes the uneducated. The Irish particularly have an uncluttered view of life and a wonderful clear channel with which to experience creativity, like humour, song, music and words.

A lot of artists have fallen by the wayside, giving up because of the recession and a huge drop in sales, but there is enormous public interest still. Artists are getting involved, free of charge, in projects like the 'Dirty Old Town' project. I will continue to paint, recession or no recession. It's a way of thinking things out. It's part of my brain. I'll scratch on stones and draw in the sand instead.

In recent years Ireland has enormously improved. At first the Celtic Tiger affected our priorities and we got consumed by money and riches. But we are back to that basic, thoughtful nature, where there is a talent to identify with those around us – the handicapped, the poor, the posh and the genius. Ireland has gone through tremendous waves in society. Pre-Celtic Tiger, there were huge religious problems. The Celtic Tiger pushed us far, but we came out of it with the veils taken from our eyes. We have become more global, but Irish people will never lose their identity. It is a gene and hopefully it will go global too.

I have two grandsons and two granddaughters and they are stunningly interested in the world. Each day I remain rooted in the present and am always open to new artistic and other challenges.

The O'Sullivan cousins from Sneem. Twins, Seán James and Daniel, twins Stella and Julia and their sister Nicole, Damien and Sam at the launch of the world record attempt at the O'Sullivan Clan Gathering.

Photograph: Don MacMonagle

Brosnan Clan Gathering.

Photograph: Dominick Walsh / Eye Focus Ltd.

Former keepers of the Hook Lighthouse, brothers Nicholas and Tux Tweedy and Martin Murphy.

Photograph: Patrick Browne

GATHERING OF LIGHTHOUSE KEEPERS
Brian O'Connell

The sea is calm, as tourists and school children queue patiently to get a look inside one of the oldest working lighthouses in the world. For over 800 years, people have looked out from Hook Head lighthouse in Co. Wexford, trying to assess the mood of the sea and warn passing ships of the rugged coastline.

Advances in modern technology means that Ireland's lighthouses are now automated and controlled centrally from the Commissioners of Irish Lights in Dún Laoghaire. But our last generation of lighthouse keepers, who were stationed in places like Hook Head, still feel a strong sense of duty towards our coastline.

They came together for a unique gathering event at Hook which featured lighthouse keepers from Ireland and across the globe.

Located on the Hook Peninsula, this 800 year-old lighthouse was built by William Marshal, Earl of Pembroke, in the early 13th century, to guide ships safely around the peninsula and its origins date back to the fifth century. It has been attended by more than 100 lighthouse keepers since around 1810.

"It is something that is always in you," explained former lighthouse keeper, Tom 'Tux' Tweedy. "I remember being on Eagle Island many years ago and it was a very bad day with a big sea. An old lighthouse keeper said to me, 'Do you know, son, the sea is a cruel mistress.' Over the last 40 years I've seen how cruel it can be, yet people can get great pleasure from it also. If you don't treat the sea properly with respect, it will turn around and bite you."

Like many lighthouse keepers, Tux comes from a family with a close attachment to the sea. Having grown up on the Hook Head peninsula, several of his brothers entered the service, and he continues to have an involvement as a lighthouse attendant at Hook Head lighthouse, where he carries out maintenance work and keeps an eye on the historic building.

"I began in 1956 as a temporary lighthouse keeper and became a principal keeper in 1990, and I remained in that position until the lighthouse became unmanned in 1996," said Tux. "Hook Head was a dwelling station until the early 1970's, and there were families living here when we were going to school. We did four hours on and eight hours off as a work routine. In the early days, before GPS, mobile and satellite phones, we were the only contact many boats had with the land. I witnessed my fair share of tragedy over the years, including one weekend in the early 1990's when five people died. You don't ever forget those times."

Tux's brother Nicholas, who was also stationed at Hook Head and other lighthouses, says that the life of a lighthouse keeper meant you could spend up to a month at a time living at some of Ireland's remotest places. Hobbies became essential to help pass the time and preserve one's sanity.

"A lot of guys did gardening or fishing. Other people had interests like putting ships in bottles, while some were painters and practically everyone read books," Nicholas said. "I was stationed at Fastnet Rock for seven years and you had to have a hobby. The introduction of television in the 1960's made a big difference to everyone of course."

Another former lighthouse keeper who grew up in lighthouses is Gerald Butler, whose father, grandfather and mother were all lighthouse keepers. Gerald is still in situ as the attendant lighthouse keeper at Galley Head lighthouse in west Cork. Growing up in a lighthouse made for an idyllic childhood as Gerald was immersed in nature and the wonders of the sea from an early age.

"I took over as a lighthouse keeper after my mother retired. I am the son of a lighthouse keeper and the grandson of a lighthouse keeper. Looking back, a lighthouse was a fantastic place to grow up in. We had 30 miles visibility in any direction and spent our time fishing or watching birds make their nests. Having moved inland now, there are trees around us, and they absolutely haunt us!"

Gerald, who was a lighthouse keeper for 21 years, was on watch in August 1979 when severe bad weather hit the bi-annual Fastnet yacht race, resulting in one of the most tragic losses of lives off our coast.

"Fastnet Rock experiences some of the worst weather we can imagine on the Irish coast," Gerald explained. "The top of the tower is 163 feet over sea level, and the kitchen is at the top. When the big storms are hitting, it puts the whole tower underneath the water and you can feel it swaying. In August 1979, as the Fastnet yacht race tragedy unfolded, we were standing on the balcony and the waves were breaking just underneath our feet. We had a big lamp and would shine it down on top of the yachts and read their sail numbers to help identify them afterwards. When the waves collapsed we could see the yachtsmen up to their knees in water, trying to hold on and battling hard. Fifteen people drowned over an eight-hour period. That was one person every half an hour. It was a terrible tragedy."

When the time came for Ireland's lighthouses to become automated in the 1990's, some lighthouse keepers found it difficult to adjust to life without their stations. "We couldn't believe it when they brought in automation," said former lighthouse keeper, Martin Murphy, who is now a county councillor in Wexford. "In our minds, we had a permanent job until we were 60. But everything just moved on, until the final sad day when we all had to accept our jobs were coming to an end, unique and different as they were. We just had to get on with life. All of us tried different things, including doing very little for a while, and that didn't work. I moved on and became an elected member of Wexford County Council, which is a different kind of choppy waters altogether!"

Ironically, though, advances in technology have given a new lease of life to Ireland's lighthouses, with many developing into well-visited tourist sites and popular locations. Through the Irish Landmark Trust, members of the public can stay overnight in some of the lighthouses no longer manned, while local communities are interacting more and more with lighthouses through events and festivals. Efforts are also under way to collate the personal testimonies of those men and women who manned the lighthouses over the generations, to ensure this fascinating aspect of our maritime heritage is preserved for the next generation.

Yvonne Shields, Chief Executive of the Commissioners of Irish Lights, said that while lighthouses are still used for navigation and maritime purposes, technology has made them more adaptable to other uses. "With advances in technology, the footprint we require to provide the maritime safety service at each lighthouse is much reduced," she said. "Those sites can now be opened up to the public for tourism and heritage. We have a strong connection to the sea in Ireland and nowhere is that more powerful than when you are standing at a lighthouse. The lighthouses have always been, and always will be, the bridge between the land and the sea."

Brian O'Connell is a journalist, author and broadcaster who contributes to The Irish Times and RTE.

The Norman Family Gathering, Werburgh Street Church, Co. Dublin.

Photograph: Seamus Travers

Pat and Maureen's legacy. Roches of Blackwater, Co. Wexford.

HOME THOUGHTS FROM ABROAD

A reflection by Dr Paddy Boland

Paddy Boland is an Irish oncologist and a senior member of the Orthopedic Oncology Service at Memorial Sloan-Kettering Cancer Center and Weill Cornell Medical School in New York.

Thirty-two years ago I moved to New York as a trainee surgeon. Like most of the Irish diaspora I still refer to Ireland as 'home' and take solace in the anticipation of *Bás in Éirinn*. It is perhaps this anticipation, and the fact that it is the year of *The Gathering*, that has prompted me to reflect on the influence Irish medicine has had on the world – and the influence the world has had on Irish medicine.

As the 'land of saints and scholars', Ireland has made a significant contribution to learning, philosophy and theology. But we should not forget also the huge impact of Ireland in the field of medicine.

The 1850's were the golden years of Irish medicine, when scholars from around the world came to Ireland to benefit from the teachings of medical giants of that century. Notable amongst them were Colles (Kilkenny); Hallaran (Cork); and Graves, Stokes, Adams and Corrigan from Dublin. Their names are eponyms, still used today for common diseases which they described.

The mid-19th century was also a time of starvation, with disease and the failure of the potato crop resulting in emigration. Successive epidemics of cholera, typhus and typhoid had devastating consequences. Practitioners such as Robert Graves revolutionised treatment of these conditions, but most patients still suffered miserable deaths. Records of the time indicate the significant humanitarian contributions by politicians such as Daniel O'Connell and Irish religious orders.

One hundred years later, Irish medicine was still having a far-reaching influence, with four medical graduates shining out. Dr Denis Burkitt, a native of Co. Fermanagh and graduate of TCD, discovered a lethal form of childhood cancer while working as a missionary surgeon in Equatorial Africa. As a result of his epidemiologic and subsequent oncologic research, this disease, which also occurs in the western world, is largely curable.

In the 1950's, Dr Jack Kyle, a graduate of Queens's University Belfast and one of the all-time greats of rugby, left Ireland to serve as a humanitarian surgeon in poorly served areas including Sumatra, Indonesia, and later Zambia. The GAA had its own medical sportsman and hero in Dr Padraig Carney, a UCD graduate from Swinford who played a pivotal role in Mayo's last two All-Ireland football victories in the early 1950's. Having been passed over for a dispensary appointment in rural Mayo, he emigrated to the US where he became a renowned obstetrician and gynaecologist and a powerful advocate for patients in California.

Meanwhile, a fourth physician was making his lasting impression on medicine in Ireland, using his knowledge as a doctor to affect social policy as Minister of Health in the Coalition Government of 1948. Dr Noel Browne introduced and executed sweeping changes in public health policies, at a time that coincided with the introduction of the antibiotic streptomycin, which resulted in the near eradication of tuberculosis in Ireland.

The end of the 20th century saw a marked increase in the number of Irish medical graduates who emigrated to the US as a result of intense lobbying of US universities by Irish medical schools. This has had far-reaching benefits for world medicine in general.

In Ireland, over 95% of professors in the major medical specialties received a substantial part of their post-doctoral medical training abroad, including those in the medical school at NUI Galway which is one of the world's leading centres for research in stem cell, regenerative medicine and breast cancer.

Dublin has regained its international reputation as a centre of medical and surgical excellence thanks to those who received training in the US and UK. Currently, two Irish university presidents are physicians, and both received post-doctoral training in the US – Hugh Brady, President of UCD and Michael Murphy, President of UCC.

Over here in the US, it is great to see that so many Irish medical graduates have risen to positions of international importance. On the east coast there is Martin Carey, Trevor

McGill and Garret Fitzgerald, all senior professors in prestigious universities. Another is Eileen O'Reilly, a TCD graduate and pioneer in the management of cancer of the liver and pancreas, with whom I have the honour of working.

On the west coast, Professor Ralph deVere White is an internationally known urologist. The renowned Mayo Clinic has several Irish-trained doctors. They include J. Aidan Carney, Emeritus Professor of Pathology, who gave his name to the complex neoplastic syndrome, and recently arrived UCD graduate, Andrew Keaveny, Chief of Hepatobiliary Medicine.

Recently a huge honour has been bestowed in the UK on Dublin-born Stephen O'Rahilly from Finglas, a UCD graduate, Professor of Clinical Biochemistry and Medicine at Cambridge University and a fellow of the Royal Society. He received a knighthood in the 2013 Queen's Birthday Honours for services to medical research.

Another Irishman, Dermot Kelleher, a former Professor of Medicine at TCD, has recently accepted the position of Principal of the Faculty of Medicine at the world-renowned Imperial College in London.

So the Irish influence on medical research is pretty clear. It is an influence that will remain strong in the future, as journeys are made backwards and forwards across the Atlantic.

And keeping with the spirit of *The Gathering,* it is fitting that some of the world's leading cancer specialists gathered in Dublin for the *Gathering Around Cancer* meeting, to discuss developments in treatments for the disease, and to map a way forward for new breakthroughs. Ireland should hold its head proud.

Rachel Collins, John Collins and Andrew Collins of Burnley, Lancashire at the disused Ballinlough, Roscommon railway station from where their father/grandfather Patrick Collins of Leatra, Williamstown bought a one way ticket to England in 1951.

Photograph: Julie Collins

CULLITON GATHERING
Laois

They came from New Orleans, Houston, New York, California, Seattle, Alberta, Spain and Scotland, all descendants of Lawrence Culliton who left Ireland in 1851.

Organised by Lawrence's great-great grandson, Rory Culliton, 140 family members spanning all ages from babes in arms to a spritely 87 year-old came to Co. Laois. They enjoyed walks in the Slieve Blooms, tours of the homesteads, Mass in Rosenallis church, a family day at Portlaoise Rugby Club and the odd round of golf.

Members of the 2012 GAA GPA All Stars tour party visited Breezy Point's Irish Community after Hurricane Sandy.
L to R: Dessie Farrell, Paul Flynn, Bernard Brogan, Colm O'Neill, Donal Óg Cusack, local home owners Terry Williams and Tim Devlin, Alan Milton, Pat Gilroy and Michael Darragh MacAuley.

Photograph:
Ray McManus / Sportsfile

HOW HURRICANE SANDY BROUGHT IRELAND AND AMERICA TOGETHER

A reflection by Niall O'Dowd

Niall O'Dowd is an Irish journalist based in the US and is the founder of the Irish Voice newspaper, Irish America magazine and irishcentral.com.

Breezy Point, New York, is a barrier inlet on the eastern tip of Queens. It has long been a haven for arriving Irish, and the generations of Irish who settled there created a strong and bonded community which never forgot its roots.

Taoiseach Enda Kenny, who came on St Patrick's weekend 2013, took part in what will surely be one of the most unusual tasks he will perform as leader. It was a unique Irish gathering, occasioned not by Americans reaching out to Ireland in a time of need, but the other way around.

He was there to accept thanks from thousands of Irish-Americans who had waited patiently for him and his party to arrive at the little Irish redoubt.

Breezy Point, by the census numbers, is the most Irish place in the US, and was also the place most devastated by Hurricane Sandy. The little community parked on the edge of Queens has no natural barriers to raging winds and high waters, and the hurricane overwhelmed them.

A flash fire had raced through this beach community, destroying over 100 houses almost instantly. Such a tale of wreckage and human despair was hard to match.

It is not the first time it was hit by tragedy. The Rockaways neighbourhood which Breezy is part of was devastated on 9/11, as the peninsula is home to hundreds of fire fighters and policemen who left that hateful day and never came back.

Now, 12 years later, Sandy had come calling and left behind a dreadful trail of carnage. The first gathering of Irish to help out the Rockaways came together at the office of the Irish Consul General, Noel Kilkenny, in New York, and was attended by 20 or so community leaders. The word went out that the Irish community would not stand idly by.

Within a few days, after a superb community organising effort, a *meitheal* of workmen and women, 500 in all, were on their way down to help Breezy and the Rockaways. They travelled by rail, bus, car and plane, with some coming from North Carolina and Ohio.

It was an amazing response: a community, led by the consulate, understanding that sending money or clothes was not enough, but that digging out basements filled with sand, helping remove mould from homes, aiding with the biggest clean-up ever, was the way to be most effective.

A few weeks later the process was repeated and the second *meitheal* day came about. It was truly a gathering of the good. Every neighbourhood – black, Italian, Jewish, Irish – had Irish volunteers helping clean up from the storm. *The New York Times* featured the Irish efforts. It was the proudest two days I can remember in recent times for the Irish community in New York – but more was to come.

The Gaelic Players Association (GPA) who had become involved in spreading GAA games in North America, called on a dozen or so of their skilled members to come out from Ireland. Many of the GPA members had visited Breezy when they played an All-Star game in New York a few weeks after Sandy, and they had been deeply impacted by the terrible scenes of destruction.

Now they were back, restoring the heart of the Breezy community – the gym and meeting hall in the local St Thomas More Catholic Church, the centre of so many activities, especially for young people.

The water had been four feet high in the gym, but through a truly herculean effort the GPA lads, helped by locals, created a sparkling new gymnasium practically overnight.

The Irish government also played their part, sending funds to organisations in the Rockaways most in need of assistance, irrespective of race or colour.

Thus, when Enda Kenny stepped into the spanking new gymnasium on that Sunday morning after attending Mass nearby, there was a massive welcome for him. As a rural politician with deep knowledge of emigration trends from his own home county, he felt right at home with the descendants of those emigrants who now flocked around him to thank him for the work of the Irish.

He mentioned that many Irish tradesmen and women were still coming down anonymously each weekend to continue helping out, and that the bond between the community and Ireland had been renewed in a wonderful and unique way.

And indeed it had. The concept of *The Gathering* was bringing people with shared memories and histories together again.

Three thousand miles from Ireland on a breezy St Patrick's Sunday, I saw those bonds being welded together again by Irish goodwill and Irish-American gratitude in a wonderful gathering.

John F. Kennedy once stated that the Irish and Americans in the geography of the heart would always be close neighbours.

Never closer in my experience than after Hurricane Sandy.

Donal Óg Cusack, Michael Darragh MacAuley, Paul Flynn and Bernard Brogan, who helped Breezy Point's Irish Community following the devastation caused by Hurricane Sandy.

Photograph: Ray McManus/ Sportsfile

*Donata Maria Roberto-Leyden
having fun at the Roscommon
Lamb Festival Family Fun Day.*

Photograph: Michelle Hurson

THE FIRST WOMAN VET
Elizabeth Clayton

As I joined with dozens of other veterinary surgeons from all over Ireland at a special gathering in Athlone as part of the Roscommon Lamb Festival, I couldn't help but feel the enormous sense of history associated with the remarkable woman we were honouring and her connection with my own village, Athleague, in Co. Roscommon.

We were paying tribute to Aleen Cust, a veterinary surgeon who blazed a trail and courageously followed her passion in life, forging a path for other women to follow.

Aleen, an English aristocrat, was born in 1868, and embarked on a career which was considered by most at the time to be inappropriate. But she overcame the many obstacles in her path and became the first female veterinary surgeon to practice in the British Isles. Aleen Cust came to live and work in Co. Roscommon and made Athleague her home.

Athleague is a quiet and peaceful place, where the River Suck flows steadily through on its way to meet the Shannon, a deceptive setting for a truly remarkable and historically captivating story.

Aleen was born into the privileged life of an English aristocratic family, but was in fact a child of the rural Irish countryside, spending her first ten years on the Smith-Barry estate near Tipperary town, where her father, Leopold Cust, was the land agent. Aleen

Aleen Cust

and her three older brothers freely enjoyed country life in the company of dogs and horses. Leopold Cust was, however, a deeply unpopular man in this area, and after his sudden death in 1878, all of the Cust family returned to England.

Aleen's battles with convention began in earnest in 1894, when she went to Edinburgh against her mother's wishes to fulfil her ambition to become a veterinary surgeon. She had tried nursing as a career but quickly knew that it was not for her. Aleen registered in college as A.I. Custance – the name of a famous jockey of the day. Once she took this step her relationship with her mother fractured, and they did not meet again. Aleen persevered despite critics in her family and among her peers. The governing body of the veterinary profession in the UK and Ireland, the Royal College of Veterinary Surgeons (RCVS), was divided and a debate began which would continue for 20 years.

However, there was one exception, Irish vet Mr William Byrne, a native of Athleague and a serving member of the Royal College. He criticised openly the closed minds of his colleagues who clung so fiercely to the status quo. He was perplexed at their objections and said, "Why any woman who loves a horse or a dog … will not be allowed to acquire a knowledge of their diseases, is a thing I cannot understand."

It was William Byrne who gave Aleen a job in his veterinary practice at Castlestrange, close to Athleague village, when she completed her studies in Edinburgh in 1900. As women were barred from entering all professions, she was not allowed to graduate and formally enter the veterinary profession.

Aleen worked tirelessly on the farms of counties Roscommon and Galway. Routine work for all rural vets was the castration of horses, obstetric work with mares and cows and tending to all sick animals. Aleen did her farm visits riding side saddle, often on a white Arab stallion. She has been described as tall and strong. At work she wore a long gabardine skirt and jacket and a man's wide brimmed hat. She clearly enjoyed her work and the people she worked with in Roscommon and Galway. She later referred to her clients as "the most horse-loving, horse-knowing, keenly critical people in the world."

Despite all the controversy raging in the background about her attempts to formally enter the profession, Aleen continued her work in Ireland. She accepted a post as Veterinary Inspector with Galway Co. Council, despite Royal College opposition. She attended veterinary conferences at home and abroad in the guise of a 'visitor', as she could not legally call herself a veterinary surgeon.

After William Byrne died prematurely in 1910, Aleen established her own veterinary practice in Athleague. She bought an estate in the village called Fort Lyster, from where she managed a farm and ran her practice. Today, the house has been demolished, but the imposing entrance pillars and the orchard walls remain. It is not difficult for visitors to imagine the busy activity at Fort Lyster, supervised by Aleen Cust.

Finally, in 1922, Aleen was allowed to take the necessary Royal College exam, and she officially became the first female veterinary surgeon in the UK and Ireland, at the age of 54. She sold her property in Athleague in 1924, and retired to England. She bought a property in Plaitford village in Hampshire, and explained to friends that it was the place that most reminded her of Roscommon. Aleen Cust died while on holiday in Jamaica in 1937.

Fast forward to the Aleen Cust gathering, which was held in the Hodson Bay Hotel in 2013. Aleen's deep connection with Athleague was noted and there was a comprehensive tour of the area that included Fort Lyster and Castlestrange. Aleen's legacy to women and the veterinary profession was discussed as well as challenges faced then and now by women in male dominated work arenas.

There are so many strands woven together in Aleen Cust's inspirational life - the struggle of women to enter areas of life that were reserved for men, the ambiguous position of the British aristocracy, who both loved and feared the Irish, and of course, the deep connection between man or woman and animals. I believe Aleen's life is best reflected in her own words: "I freely admit that the best of my fun I owe it to the horse and hound".

Elizabeth Clayton helped organise this Gathering with fellow vets Gerard Browne, Miriam Finn, Eimear Fitzgerald and Catherine O'Roarke.

(Below left)
Winners of the Bo Peep &
Boy Blue Competition Micheal
Shriane and Adrina Gallagher
at the Roscommon Lamb
Festival Family Fun Day.

(Below right)
Ciaran O'Shea with the
European Eagle Owl at the
Roscommon Lamb Festival.

Photographs: Michelle Hurson

Photograph:
Malcolm McGettigan/
BigOMedia

THE NEW IRISH
A reflection by Carl O'Brien

Carl O'Brien is a journalist with The Irish Times.

The make-up of the Irish population today is starkly different to anything witnessed by previous generations. There are more nationalities, more languages and more ethnicities than ever before. There are many 'new Irish' who now call Ireland home. They have put down roots, their children go to school here and they have formed part of the community in every city, town and village across the State.

Ethnic diversity is now an established fact of Irish life rather than a passing trend that will be reversed by the chill winds of the recession. The accession of eastern and central European countries to the European Union almost a decade ago, along with the economic boom, were the biggest drivers of demographic change on this island. Many suspected this population growth was temporary and that foreigners would leave once the economy declined. But Ireland – like many other developed countries before it – is learning that immigration is not just a temporary phenomenon.

Change can be challenging. New research shows that Irish opposition to immigration has spiked since the recession began. Some campaigners fear a growth in the types of racial tension that has plagued other European countries. Campaigners say this is why there is an urgent need to adopt an integration policy to ensure migrants don't get isolated.

But overall, the story of immigration is immensely positive. Our culture is being enriched. Pathways to citizenship mean that for many families the country is happy to accept our new arrivals as full members of society.

ZEPHYRIN NGALIEMA, DEMOCRATIC REPUBLIC OF CONGO

The first thing I thought of when I heard the name Dublin was 'romance'. Why? There was a movie I had seen years earlier, *Les Roses de Dublin*. It conjured up such a nice image in my head. Apart from that, not many people in the Democratic Republic of the Congo knew much about Ireland.

I had to leave my legal firm behind for security reasons. I wanted to go somewhere safe, and where I could work and raise my family. That wasn't possible at home. That's how I ended up here six years ago.

My first impressions of Ireland were mixed. Not long after I arrived, I was walking down O'Connell Street and these crazy kids were calling me names. Soon, I realised that it was a very small minority of people – it wasn't representative of the wider population.

Lot of things attracted me. The weather was mild and public officials treated us fairly, a big difference to the corruption at home. After six months or so, my wife and two children were able to join me. She left her dental practice at home.

There are some frustrations: I would love to work as a lawyer, but my qualifications aren't recognised here. That's why I do volunteer work for immigrants. My wife would also like to put her experience as a dentist to good work, but must go back to college to gain new qualifications.

Overall, I feel my future is here. We're so proud to be naturalised Irish.

ANN ELIZABETH GUAN, PHILIPPINES

I'm here around ten years now. It has been a challenging time. I work as a carer and, like many people, earn close to the minimum wage. The money for these kinds of jobs used to be much better, but the pay has gone down. It makes it much more difficult to save enough money to send to my family in the Philippines.

I have four children at home. The money I send is for their education, for food, but also to pay the mortgage on the house. There isn't the kind of social safety net at home that there is in Europe, so you have to pay for everything.

I have a long-term residency permit, which makes a very big difference; it gives me a real sense of security. It also makes you less dependent on work permits, which last for just one or two years.

I was out of work for quite a while in Ireland, which meant I had to use up all of my savings. That's very frustrating. I'm back to where I was. It doesn't get any easier, but I have to go on.

Most of my friends over here are from the Philippines. They are also supporting their families at home. They work in different types of caring: nursing homes, childcare, that kind of thing. It's more common for them to have negative experiences, I find. You need trust with an employer — it's very important.

PETER SZLOVAK, HUNGARY

There are days when I feel like I'm really at home. Recently, I was in a pub in Rathmines, and there were traditional musicians singing and people of all nationalities. I sang *Do You Want Your Aul' Lobby Washed Down?* Everyone stopped to listen. I felt I belonged.

I first came here in 2003 for six months. I was doing some voluntary work in a residential home for people with disabilities. It was a chance to go abroad and learn a language. What struck me at the beginning was that it felt like a young society. There was a sense of freedom and people enjoying new-found prosperity.

I think the Irish public thought, "All these people are just passing through." The big surprise was when the recession came and so many people opted to stay.

There are things which I still find unusual. If you don't drink, it's way more difficult to socialise, but maybe that is changing. And people tend to avoid conflict at all costs, which can be good — and bad.

Ireland has been having a hard time. There is huge dissatisfaction with the government and the banks. I think that people here will learn a lot from what happened — and make sure it doesn't happen again.

GREG STRATON, SOUTH AFRICA

I arrived here in my early 20s with my suitcase, €300 in my pocket and a handful of CVs. I had heard there were good work opportunities here. The first thing that struck me was the attitude: people didn't take things too seriously, it was much more informal. I liked that.

I wanted to work at something that was socially conscious, so I ended up with a group — Spirasi — that supports asylum seekers, migrants and refugees here. It felt like my calling.

Once you get beyond the initial welcome, it can be difficult to get real acceptance. It took a while, but I found that it came when I got more involved in structured things like walking clubs and swimming. I got an allotment, which was a good way of meeting people.

Ireland now feels like home. I met my partner here and my son is going to school. Some people wonder about Ireland's welcoming reputation – but it's deserved. There is a genuine interest in people here. The big challenge now is how to deal with immigration in the long term. I think people are scared to talk about these issues, for fear of being branded racists. If there's a vacuum, that can be dangerous. What kind of society do people want? Is there too much pressure placed on poorer communities? All these questions need to be debated.

ROTIMI ADEBARI, NIGERIA

When the Mayor's chain of office was placed on my shoulders in County Hall, Portlaoise, in 2007, I became the first black man to be elected Mayor of an Irish town. I believe this story is proof that the Ireland of 100,000 welcomes is a living reality and not just a piece of marketing.

I first heard of the *céad míle fáilte* from an Irish priest in my native Nigeria. Fleeing religious persecution, I arrived in Ireland with my wife Ronke and two children, aged eight and four. It would be true to say that not everybody had a warm welcome, but for every Irish person pulling you down there are 100 to lift you up.

Becoming an Irish citizen in 2009 was very important for me and my wife. We have two children who were born here and our two older children are citizens. Ireland is our home, it is the place that made us welcome and gave us a new life.

Having seen Ireland in 'boom and bust' I am confident that the capacity of Irish people, new and old, to work together will see the country rise again.

(From an interview between Rotimi Adebari and journalist Jim O'Brien)

Maeve Martin Kelly, Sossena and her twin brother Sofoneas Hilbert from Muelheim an der Ruhr, Germany at the Taste of Adare which kicked off a year of gatherings at the Adare Heritage Centre.

Photograph: Seán Curtin

Robert Ballagh

2013 is a very important year, not just because of The Gathering, but because it marks the 100th anniversary of the 1913 Lockout, a major turning point in Irish industrial relations history.

I was delighted to work on the 1913 Lockout Tapestry with fellow artist, Cathy Henderson. It is not in fact a tapestry, but that is the word we are using, as it's a word the general public understand.

A true tapestry is completely woven, but this project involves a variety of techniques — embroidery, patchwork, appliqué and so on. It is made up of almost 30 panels. The panel pictured here shows Dublin Metropolitan Policemen baton-charging the crowd on Sackville Street during the Lockout — an incident later called 'Bloody Sunday'.

The 1913 Lockout Tapestry was commissioned by SIPTU and the National College of Art and Design to tell the story of the Lockout.

Each panel in the tapestry is physically created by members of different organisations, including the Irish Embroidery Guild, Irish Patchwork Society, ICA, and a number of community and prison groups. It is overseen by Angela Keane of the National College of Art and Design.

245

*Finding the deep heart's core
at Fanore Beach, Co. Clare. The
University of Wisconsin Literary
Tour of Ireland.*

Photograph: Marguerite Helmers